LIVING STONES

PEBBLES

LIVING STONES

PEBBLES

SUSAN SAYERS

**Illustrated by
Arthur Baker**

Kevin
Mayhew

First published in 1997 by
KEVIN MAYHEW LTD
Rattlesden
Bury St Edmunds
Suffolk IP30 0SZ

0 1 2 3 4 5 6 7 8 9

ISBN 1 84003 010 0
Catalogue No. 1500114

The other titles in the *Living Stones* series are

Complete Resource Book	ISBN 1 84003 009 7	Cat. No. 1500113
Prayers of Intercession	ISBN 1 84003 013 5	Cat. No. 1500117
Rocks	ISBN 1 84003 011 9	Cat. No. 1500115
Boulders	ISBN 1 84003 012 7	Cat. No. 1500116

Cover photographs:
Two small children – courtesy of SuperStock Ltd, London
Background – courtesy of Images Colour Library Ltd, London
Cover design by Jaquetta Sergeant
Edited by Katherine Laidler
Typesetting by Louise Hill
Printed in Great Britain

FOREWORD

For this age group the world is opening out from the immediate family circle, and full of possibilities. The children are becoming aware of familiar faces Sunday by Sunday, and now they are brought in to join the big children for Sunday school. It can be a daunting prospect, and the way young children are met and welcomed, talked and listened to, when they first encounter the children's ministry in your church, will have profound effect on their spiritual growth. It is through the good humour, care and friendliness of those they meet that they will begin to realise how God loves them.

In all your planning, keep aware of how it will seem from the children's point of view. Is the area attractive and inviting? Does the furniture fit? Is the atmosphere orderly and therefore unthreatening? Are people talking at a speed they can cope with, and giving them time to reply without pressure? Do people genuinely seem to like them and want them to be happy? Is considerate love and fairness expressed in actions as well as in the teaching? Is it a place where they can relax and feel at home? Is it fun?

These things are so important because the children will be learning far more from the way things are done and from the people they work with, than from the actual teaching content, valuable as this obviously is. It is a good idea to review your aims and objectives annually, setting out for yourselves, the PCC, the parents, and any helpers, what you are doing and why, what works well and what needs to be tried differently. If this regular review is built into the system there is no danger of outdated methods carrying on past their sell-by date just because things have always been done like that. A termly or annual training day is also helpful in refreshing leaders and preventing cases of burn-out.

This book provides you with ideas and materials for activities for young children, all based on the RCL weekly readings. The activity sheets often include something to think and talk about together, and you can select and adapt the ideas to suit your particular group. Vary the media the children work with – crayons, finger paints, sponge painting, printing, paper and fabric collage, chalks and pastels are all fun to use. Pray for the children and their families, and read the Bible passages before you plan, so as to incorporate your own valuable insights, and use the suggested games either as they stand or as starting points to help you think of other ideas of your own.

A few general ideas about story-telling:

- Tell the story from the viewpoint of a character in the situation. To create the time-machine effect, avoid eye contact as you slowly put on the appropriate cloth or cloak, and then make eye contact as you greet the children in character.

- Have an object with you which leads into the story – a water jug, or a lunch box, for instance.

- Walk the whole group through the story, so that they are physically moving from one place to another; and use all kinds of places, such as broom cupboards, under the stairs, outside under the trees, and so on.

- Collect some carpet tiles – blue and green – so that at story time the children can sit round the edge of this and help you place on the cut-outs for the story.

If parents are going to be staying with their children, involve them in the activities, or think over the possibility of having an adult discussion group in the same room, using the study material and discussion questions in the *Living Stones* Complete Resource Book. Parents are encouraged to pray with their children during the week, using the worksheet prayers.

All the material in the book is copyright-free for non-commercial use in churches and schools.

SUSAN SAYERS

CONTENTS

ORDINARY TIME

RECOMMENDED BIBLES

It is often a good idea to look at a passage in several different versions before deciding which to use for a particular occasion.

As far as children are concerned, separate Bible stories, such as those published by Palm Tree Press and Lion, are a good introduction for the very young. Once children are reading, a very helpful version is the *International Children's Bible* (New Century version) published by Word Publishing. Here children have a translation based on experienced scholarship, using language structure suitable for young readers, with short sentences and appropriate vocabulary. There is a helpful dictionary, and clear maps and pictures are provided.

CHRISTMAS DAY

Christmas Day is very much a time for all God's children to worship together, and I have not included separate ideas or worksheets for the children. Use and adapt some of the all-age suggestions in the *Living Stones* Complete Resource Book, and have nativity toys, such as knitted Mary, Joseph and Jesus, shepherds and sheep, for the very youngest to play with in the toddlers' area.

Although worksheets and ideas are provided for Mothering Sunday and Easter Day, these are also times for celebrating and learning together.

ADVENT

FIRST SUNDAY OF ADVENT

Thought for the day

The gathered hopes of generations remind us to get ourselves ready, so that Christ's return will be a day of excitement and great joy.

Readings

Jeremiah 33:14-16
Psalm 25:1-10
1 Thessalonians 3:9-13
Luke 21:25-36

Aim

To help them understand getting ready for Christmas in terms of getting ready to meet Jesus in person.

Starter

Stop . . . Get ready . . . Go! Starting always from standing still in a space on their own, on the word 'Go!' the children do whatever the leader calls out (e.g. hop like rabbits, swim around like fish, slither like snakes). When the leader calls 'Stop!' the children stop and at 'Get ready!' they go to the starting position again.

Teaching

Draw their attention to the way they had to get ready for the game each time. Christmas is coming – whose birthday is it at Christmas? How are we going to get ready for Christmas?

Jesus told us that one day he would come back. We will be able to see him, either then or when we die, whichever happens first.

How can we get ready to meet Jesus? What would he like to see us doing?

During the discussion, make simple drawings of the way they think Jesus would like to see them living.

Praying

The children find a space on their own again. Taking the ideas they have come up with, lead the children to pray: 'Jesus, we want to be ready to meet you. Please help us to . . . (share our toys/forgive each other/be kind to our brothers and sisters, etc.)', and everyone mimes the activity. Then call out 'Stop!' and the children go back to their space for the next prayer.

Activities

Use the worksheet to reinforce the idea of getting ready for Christmas being linked with getting ready to meet Jesus.

Notes

Jesus is coming

Here I am getting ready for Jesus.

Here I am getting ready for Christmas.

Weeks to Christmas

4 3 2 1

For parents and children together. This week's prayer

Dear Jesus, thank you for loving us so much. Amen.

a brush

some brown paint

POSTER COLOUR

Get ready to paint!

We are starting to make a Christmas crib today.
You will need a box.

Next week we will make the manger.

SECOND SUNDAY OF ADVENT

Thought for the day

It had been prophesied that there would be a messenger to prepare the way for the coming of the Messiah. Now John the Baptist appears with his urgent message of repentance.

Readings

Malachi 3:1-4
Canticle: Benedictus
Philippians 1:3-11
Luke 3:1-6

Aim

To understand that John was the messenger helping people get ready for Jesus.

Starter

Call and change. Sit round in a circle. One person calls someone else's name and these two change places. The one who was called becomes the next caller. This game helps build the group together, and is an acting-out of what John the Baptist was doing.

Teaching

Find out if any of the children have cousins, and what their names are. Point out that they may not live with you but they are members of your family.

Tell them that one of Jesus' cousins was John. And God had a job he needed John to do. When John was grown up God asked him to go and get people ready for Jesus.

How could he do that? First he went off on his own to pray. Then he started talking to the people. He said to them, 'Listen, I've got a message for you!'

'A message for us?' asked the people. 'What message have you got for us?'

'Well,' said John, 'we all need to get ready. Soon God will be coming to us, and we aren't ready for him yet.'

'How exciting!' said the people. 'You are right, we must be ready to welcome him. But what can we do?'

John said, 'God will want to find that we are kind and loving and being fair to one another.'

'Oh dear!' said the people. 'I'm afraid we're not always like that. Some of us have bad tempers and some of us are greedy and some of us want our own way all the time. But we do want to be ready. Please help us get ready.'

'All you have to do,' said John, 'is to be sorry about those things and want to put them right.'

'We are sorry,' said the people. 'We don't want to be bad tempered and greedy and wanting our own way all the time. We want to make God happy when he comes.'

'In that case,' said John, 'I will wash you in the river as a sign that your bad temper and greediness and wanting your own way all the time are washed away and you are forgiven.'

The people felt happy and free. They went back home to enjoy loving and sharing and being fair. It would not be easy, but they were determined to do their best.

Praying

Ask the children to sit with their hands closed up as if they are hiding something inside. Imagine that one hand holds something for which you want to thank God that you are good at. As you open that hand, think of showing the thing you are good at to God. Everyone says, 'Thank you, God, for making me good at this.' Imagine that in the other hand you are holding something you would like to be better at (telling the truth/being a good friend/helping at home). As you open this hand, think of showing God and say, 'Please, God, help me to be better at this.'

Activities

Use the worksheet to continue getting the crib ready for Christmas – today is the manger – and reinforce the teaching about John the Baptist.

Notes

Weeks to Christmas

John helps us to get ready

Parents and children together at home.

A prayer when you open each Advent calendar window.

Dear God thank you for loving us so much. Amen.

We are getting our Christmas crib ready. You will need

☐ crayons

☐ a box

☐ yellow paper

☐ scissors

Jesus and John were cousins and played together.

'Your life is washed clean.'

THIRD SUNDAY OF ADVENT

Thought for the day

Our period of preparation shifts from repentance and forgiveness to the freed exhilaration of hope, as the momentous truth of God's immanence begins to dawn on us.

Readings

Zephaniah 3:14-20
Canticle: Isaiah 12:2-6
Philippians 4:4-7
Luke 3:7-18

Aim

To celebrate looking forward to Christmas as a time of God's love being shown to us.

Starter

I'm thinking of someone . . . Everyone sits in a circle and tries to guess who you are thinking of. Start with something that could refer to lots of children (he's a boy/wearing a sweater) and gradually get more specific (his shoes have green dinosaurs on the bottom) until lots of children know who you mean. Everyone says, 'God made Jack and God loves Jack.'

Teaching

Have ready a good quality picture of the nativity (from a Christmas card) and put it in a box. Wrap the box in Christmas paper. We will use this during the teaching.

Get out some wrapping paper and scissors, and let the children guess what they are used for. Talk about why we give each other presents at Christmas, and establish that it isn't because we want something back but because we love the people and want them to see that we love them.

Now remind them of the starter activity and how God knows and loves each of us. Explain that at the first Christmas he gave the world the best Christmas present ever, not because he wanted anything back, but just because he loves us so much. Show the Christmas present. What was God's Christmas present to the world, to show he loves us? Open the present and let the children see that it is Jesus.

Praying

As you hold the Christmas present and then open it and hold up the picture, say this prayer together:

Thank you, God,
for loving the world so much
that you gave us Jesus
to be with us for ever. Amen.

Activities

Use the worksheet to continue getting ready for Christmas by making the crib – this week it's Mary, Joseph and Jesus. The present-wrapping activity will need a variety of small pieces of Christmas paper.

Notes

Weeks to Christmas

4 3 2 1

We give presents to show we love someone.

Can you wrap these presents?

Jesus

Colour Mary, Joseph and Jesus.

Cut them out.

Stick them on the wall.

We are getting ready for Christmas!

You will need

glue

crayons

scissors

At home . . .

Thank you, God, for loving the world so much that you gave us Jesus to be with us for ever. Amen.

Fourth Sunday of Advent

Thought for the day

When we co-operate with God amazing things happen.

Readings

Micah 5:2-5a
Canticle: Magnificat or Psalm 80:1-7
Hebrews 10:5-10
Luke 1:39-45 (46-55)

Aim

To understand that Mary was happy to work with God.

Starter

Working together. Ask the children to help you do various jobs as you get ready for the session. If you have access to a parachute, play some parachute games which need everyone to work together (such as 'mushroom', 'roll the ball' or tent making). Alternatively have everyone helping to make a 'Happy Christmas' frieze for the church.

Teaching

Point out how we all worked together in that activity. What jobs do they help with at home? Each time emphasise the co-operation that gets the job done well.

Use rag dolls or cut-out figures to tell the story.

God needed a very important job done. He needed someone to bring Jesus into our world and look after him. So he looked around and saw just the right person: Mary. He didn't choose her because she was rich or pretty or clever. He chose her because she was ready to work with God. She was already friends with him. She talked to him and listened to him in her prayers each day, and tried to live as God wanted her to. (How was that?)

So one day God told her he had chosen her to be the mother of Jesus. Mary was very surprised. It was such an important job, and she knew it would be a hard job to do well. What do you think – did she say yes or no?

Mary said 'Yes!' and went off to visit her cousin Elizabeth who lived in another town. Elizabeth was going to have a baby, too. You remember John the Baptist we met last week? Well, it was him, only he hadn't been born yet when Mary went to see his mother.

As soon as they met they hugged and kissed, and John started leaping about inside his mum because he was so excited! (Have you ever felt a baby moving about inside your mum? It's a funny feeling.)

Mary didn't need to tell Elizabeth her news. Elizabeth seemed to know already, and they sang and danced to praise God for being so wonderful.

Praying

Leader Dear God,
when you want us to be kind, help us to say

All Yes!

Leader When you want us to be honest, help us to say

All Yes!

Leader When you want us to help someone, help us to say

All Yes!

Activities

The worksheet helps the children to complete their Christmas crib today, so these can be blessed in church and taken home. They are also going over the main points of today's story.

Notes

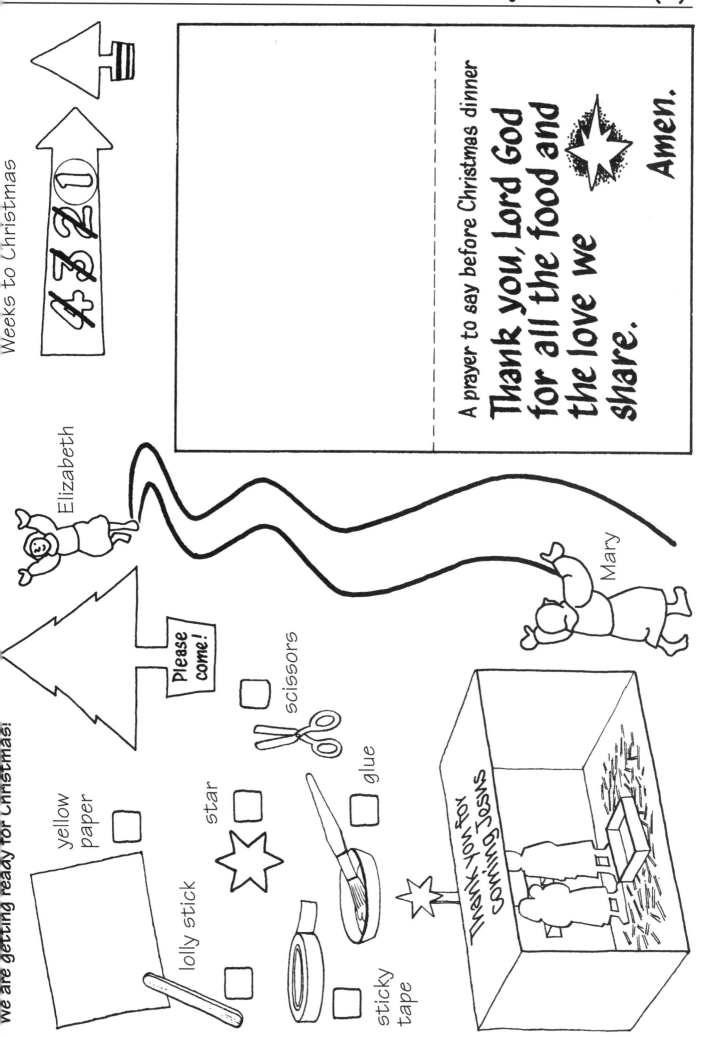

Weeks to Christmas

4 3 2 0

Elizabeth

Mary

we are getting ready for Christmas!

yellow paper

lolly stick

star

scissors

glue

sticky tape

Please come!

A prayer to say before Christmas dinner

Thank you, Lord God for all the food and the love we share.

Amen.

Thank you for coming Jesus

CHRISTMAS

FIRST SUNDAY OF CHRISTMAS

Thought for the day

Jesus' perception and understanding of his purpose and work begins to take shape throughout his childhood.

Readings

1 Samuel 2:18-20, 26
Psalm 148
Colossians 3:12-17
Luke 2:41-52

Aim

To get to know the story of Jesus being lost and found.

Starter

Play hide and seek in small groups so that everyone gets the chance both to hide and be found.

Teaching

Talk about how it felt to be looking for the hidden children and how it felt to find them. Today's story is about a time when Mary and Joseph went looking for Jesus.

Using the 'carpet tiles and cut outs' method tell the story of the visit to Jerusalem with all the mums and dads and children and uncles and aunties and grandparents and cousins. Jesus was twelve years old. Give all the children a cut-out donkey or camel to add to the trail of visitors going up to Jerusalem. Pictures to use in the story are given with the worksheet.

When everyone sets off for home all the trail of animals can be turned over to face the other way, and then Mary and Joseph's donkey will turn back again to find Jesus, before finally joining the others.

Praying

When we are sitting still *(sit still)*:
   we know you are with us, Jesus.
When we are walking along *(walk along)*:
   we know you are with us, Jesus.
When we are playing *(play)*:
   we know you are with us, Jesus.
When we are helping *(pretend to help clean or tidy up)*:
   we know you are with us, Jesus. Amen.

Activities

The worksheet has a searching to find activity and consolidates the main points of the story. The children can also talk over what to do if they ever lose their mum or dad when they are out shopping.

Notes

Jesus is lost . . . .

Stick the picture of Jesus where Mary and Joseph found him in the end.

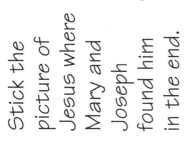

. . . and found

For parents

Your child has been thinking about what to do if they get lost. Can you fill in the details that apply in your particular family?

To pray together

When we are sitting still (sit still) we know you are with us, Jesus.
When we are walking along (walk along) we know you are with us, Jesus.

(Add other verses like brushing our teeth, driving to Nana's, shopping, cleaning the car, etc.)

Cut out Jesus. Where did Mary and Joseph find him?

Can you see them?

?

SECOND SUNDAY OF CHRISTMAS

Thought for the day

Christ is the way God tells people about himself.

Readings

Jeremiah 31:7-14
Psalm 147:12-20
Ephesians 1:3-14
John 1:(1-9) 10-18

Aim

To help them understand that God shows us he loves us by coming to live with us.

Starter

Have some raisins or chocolate buttons which you hand round to each child in turn, by name. Point out that you are fond of them, and wanted to show them by giving them a little something. God loves each of us by name, and he had a very good idea for showing us his love.

Teaching

One day God was looking at all the world he had made. He smelt the roses, laughed at the monkeys playing in the trees, smiled to himself as a child helped his baby brother to play football, and enjoyed the beautiful sunset. It was a very good world.

Then he got sad as he watched an owner hitting a dog, two children fighting, and a grown-up stealing some money. God had made people able to choose right or wrong, and lots of them were choosing wrong instead of right, even though God knew it would make them happier to choose right.

The trouble was that although he was there, the people couldn't see him. No one can see God. And God longed to help them.

One day he decided to become a human himself and live among them. 'And then,' thought God, 'they will understand how to live. They will be able to follow my example, and I will help them.'

Well, of course God couldn't stop being God and be a human instead – if he did that all the world would come to a sudden and nasty end.

So this is what God did. He spoke his great love for the world and his longing for the people, and the great love he spoke became a human baby, all ready to grow up in a human family, and show all the people what God was really like.

And do you know the name of that baby, born from the word of great love that God spoke? The baby's name was Jesus, and we have just been celebrating his birthday! Jesus is God saying 'I love you'.

Praying

Jesus, you show us what God is like.
You show us that he loves us.
Thank you, Jesus! Amen.

Activities

On the worksheet there are instructions for making a frame to put on a mirror. Whoever looks into the mirror will see someone God loves. There is also a dot-to-dot which helps us see something we couldn't see before and a picture which reinforces the teaching.

Notes

1 Colour the frame
2 Cut out the middle
3 Stick it on shiny mirror paper
4 Let your family and friends
  look in it

You will need

glue

crayons

scissors

paper

For parents

Look for things God has
made which are good/faithful.
Read some stories of Jesus.
Pray with your child.

Jesus, you show us
what God is like.
You show us that
he loves us.
Thank you, Jesus.
Amen.

Jesus is God
saying

I ♥ you!

Who is hidden here? Join the dots to see it.

God is
hidden, too.
But we can
see him in
Jesus.

EPIPHANY

THE EPIPHANY

Thought for the day

Jesus, the hope of the nations, is shown to the world.

Readings

Isaiah 60:1-6
Psalm 72:(1-9) 10-15
Ephesians 3:1-12
Matthew 2:1-12

Aim

To become familiar with the story of the wise men finding Jesus.

Starter

Play pass the parcel. At the different layers have old bus and train tickets. The prize at the end is a star-shaped biscuit.

Teaching

Tell the children that today we are going to hear about a journey. It isn't a bus journey or a car journey or a train journey. This is a camel journey. (All pack your bags and get on your camels.) We are very wise people, but we don't know where we are going. We are looking for a baby king. And we are packing presents for him. (Pack gold, frankincense and myrrh.) Produce a star on a stick as you explain how a special star has started shining in the sky and we are sure it will lead us to the baby king. Lead off behind the star, riding your camels, and pretending to go over high mountains, through water, stopping for the night, and going to sleep and so on. At last you reach the town of Bethlehem (stick up a sign) where you find the baby king with his mum and dad. (Have a large picture, or one of the cribs made before Christmas.) We all get off our camels and give the baby our presents. The baby's name is Jesus and we have found him at last!

Praying

This is a prayer the wise men might have said. We have all been invited to find Jesus as well, so we can say it with them.

Thank you, Jesus,
for inviting me
to come and look for you.
I am glad I have found you! Amen.

Activities

To emphasise that the journey of the wise men was probably a hard one, there is a maze to help the wise men find their way to Bethlehem. The star-making activity will need star templates, and ready-cut card for the younger children.

Notes

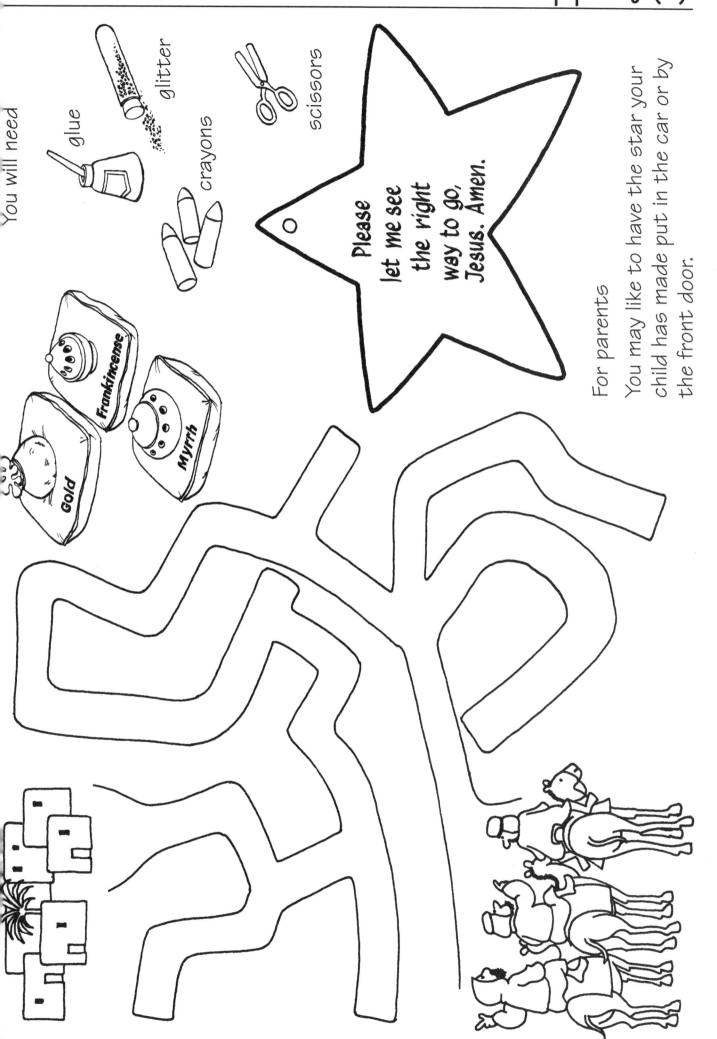

You will need

glue

glitter

crayons

scissors

Frankincense

Gold

Myrrh

Please
let me see
the right
way to go,
Jesus. Amen.

For parents
You may like to have the star your child has made put in the car or by the front door.

THE BAPTISM OF CHRIST: FIRST SUNDAY OF EPIPHANY

Thought for the day

Jesus is baptised, and God confirms his identity and his calling.

Readings

Isaiah 43:1-7
Psalm 29
Acts 8:14-17
Luke 3:15-17, 21-22

Aim

To know that God knows them by name.

Starter

Have a number of pictures or objects set out in the middle of the circle. The children guess the name you are thinking of by the way you describe the object or picture. Start with more general statements and get more specific, like this: 'I'm thinking of something which is round . . . and white . . . and you might put cornflakes in it.' They have to say the name, rather than pointing, unless they are very young.

Teaching

Have the children's names written out carefully on cards with a string attached so they can be worn. Hold up each one in turn and describe the person the name belongs to, by nature as well as looks, and with lots of positives. The children can join in by adding things they like about each one. When all the children are wearing their names, tell them how God knows each of us by name. He already knows all the things about us that we have talked about, and lots more as well.

Show a picture of a baby, a child, and an adult being baptised, and talk about God calling us by name to follow him. They may remember a Christening in the family, or one of the recent ones in church, and can tell the others what happened. Have a jug and a bowl of water so they can focus on that as they hear about Baptism.

Praying

Dear God,
you know my name
and you know me
and you love me.
I know your name.
I know you and I love you!

Activities

The name cards can be decorated with coloured sticky paper, finger-painting or with pens. On the sheet there are objects and people to name, and thank God for, and space to draw themselves doing something they like doing.

Notes

This is my name

This
is me
doing
what I like
best

Can you name these?

Dear God,
you know my name
and you know me
and you love me.
I know your name.
I know you and
I love you!

SECOND SUNDAY OF EPIPHANY

Thought for the day

As a marriage celebrates the beginning of a changed, new life for the bride and groom, so our loving, faithful God has chosen us and is ready to transform our lives for the good of the world.

Readings

Isaiah 62:1-5
Psalm 36:5-10
1 Corinthians 12:1-11
John 2:1-11

Aim

To be introduced to the story of the wedding at Cana.

Starter

Water play. Protect the floor and have a number of washing-up bowls with water, containers and sieves. Let the younger children enjoy filling and emptying. Older children can be encouraged to see how many small containers it takes to fill a larger one.

Teaching

Talk with the children about any weddings they may have been to and taken part in. Show a few wedding photos (preferably amateur ones which show people enjoying themselves rather than in set poses). Now tell them about the time Jesus and his mother were invited to a wedding. When you get to the part about the water jars, fill a large jug with water. Pour some into a wine glass as you tell them about the servants pouring it out. The fact that it is of course still water can lead on to what happened in Cana. I think this is far preferable to the red colouring stunts which only turn it all into a magic trick.

Praying

Thank you for the falling rain.

wiggle fingers downwards

Thank you for the rising sap.

draw fingers upwards over body, as if a tree

Thank you for the juicy fruit.

hold arms out with fingers hanging down

Thank you for my favourite fruity drink! Amen.

pretend to drink it

Activities

On the worksheet they will be changing things and making them special, and this forms a basis for thinking about how God works in our lives. Instructions for making a clay or plasticine water pot are given on the sheet.

Notes

Can you change

Can you change   Can you change

into a picture of someone you love?

How to make a clay or plasticine water jar.

1   2   3

into a king?

into a plate with your favourite food?

Water

Wine

wine

water

Colour this red and cut it out. Put it over the water as you tell the story.

Can you show what Jesus did to the water?

THIRD SUNDAY OF EPIPHANY

Thought for the day

The meaning of the scriptures is revealed to the people.

Readings

Nehemiah 8:1-3, 5-6, 8-10
Psalm 19
1 Corinthians 12:12-31a
Luke 4:14-21

Aim

For them to develop listening skills, both physically and spiritually.

Starter

Listen for your name. Sit in a circle. Have a plate of pieces of fruit and tell the children that one by one they can choose a piece to eat. You will call their name when it's their turn. For each one you can say something like, 'Max, you can jump to choose a piece of fruit now. Imogen, you can crawl to choose a piece of fruit now.' Speaking our name alerts us to listen, and God knows us by name.

Teaching

Give out percussion instruments (home-made shakers will be fine) to everyone and have a quiet bell yourself. Get everyone to play loudly, along with a track from a praise tape. Stop everyone and ask if anyone could hear the little bell. Play it on its own so they know what to listen for and then get everyone playing again, but listening out for the bell. Now collect all the instruments in and give the bell to a child to play while we all listen. Now it sounds quite clear, but before, when we were all making a noise, it was so quiet we could hardly hear it.

Stand at one end of the room facing the wall, and see if the children can creep up on you without you hearing them.

Sit in the circle again and try passing the bell (or a crackly, rustly bag) around the circle without it making any noise at all. All these things develop listening skills, both the attentiveness and concentration and also the body control. Praise the children for their success as some will find this quite a challenge. Tell the children how God helps us to know if something is right or wrong, and show this using puppets. Just as a puppet is thinking aloud about stealing something, or telling a lie or being unkind, ring the little bell. The puppet realises that something is wrong, and changes his/her action.

Explain that God never forces us to make the right choice (that's for us to decide) but he does let us know what is right, to help us make the right choice.

Praying

Jesus, when you say

Stop! Think! Change! *(ring the bell three times)*

Help me to hear you *(hands on ears)*

and help me to do it. Amen. *(hands out, palms up)*

Activities

The worksheet helps the children to explore how we hear best, both physically and spiritually. The instruments can then be used to make a storm, starting very quiet, building up and then dying away into silence.

Notes

What is God saying?

For parents

Help your child to play a listening game this week. Here is a prayer to pray together.

Jesus, when you say,
STOP! THINK! CHANGE!
Help me to hear you and help me to do it.
Amen.

God lets us know what is right and what is wrong

(but we do need to listen!)

Look at this picture. Edward is trying to tell his mum some news. Why can't she hear him?

Draw them in a quiet place so Edward can tell his news and his mum can hear it.

FOURTH SUNDAY OF EPIPHANY

Thought for the day

At eight days old, Jesus is presented in the temple, and at the Purification is revealed to Simeon and Anna as the promised Saviour who is able to reveal to us our true selves.

Readings

Ezekiel 43:27–44:4
Psalm 48
1 Corinthians 13:1-13
Luke 2:22-40

Aim

To know that Simeon had been waiting for the Saviour and knew it was Jesus.

Starter

A waiting game. Everyone gets into a space and sits down. The leader calls out, 'Ready . . . steady . . . hop/jump/walk!' and the children mustn't move until they have heard the full instruction. You can make it harder by sometimes giving the instruction quickly and sometimes slowly. Today we are going to meet someone who waited all his life for something, but at last he got it.

Teaching

Dress up one of the leaders as Simeon, or just tell the children we have a visitor today, and put on a head-dress and white beard as they watch. When you are ready, resume eye contact with them and say, 'Hallo, children, my name's Simeon. Can you say, "Hallo, Simeon"?' Say you want to tell them about something exciting that happened to you. Tell them how old you are, and explain that you love God and know you can trust him. You knew that one day God was going to send someone to save and rescue people, and God had told you that you would see this Saviour in person before you died. Go on to tell the children what happened on that day in the temple when Joseph and Mary brought Jesus in. Chat your story, involving the children, and try to get across your excitement at actually meeting the Saviour God had promised.

Praying

Leader   Simeon knew he could trust God.

All   We can trust God, too.

Leader   Simeon loved God.

All   We love God, too.

Leader   Simeon knew that Jesus had come to save us.

All   We know Jesus came to save us, too.

Activities

The worksheet goes over the story with a sequencing activity involving cutting and sticking. If you have nativity dressing-up clothes suitable for the children they can 'play' the story through in costume.

Notes

Join the dots to see something that helps you see in the dark.

How is Jesus a light for us?

He helps us see the way to live.

For parents

At home you can help your child stick this prayer on the back of their story, and then pray it together.

Parent	Simeon knew he could trust God
Child/Parent	We can trust God, too
Parent	Simeon loved God
Child/Parent	We love God, too
Parent	Simeon knew that Jesus had come to save us
Child/Parent	We know Jesus came to save us, too

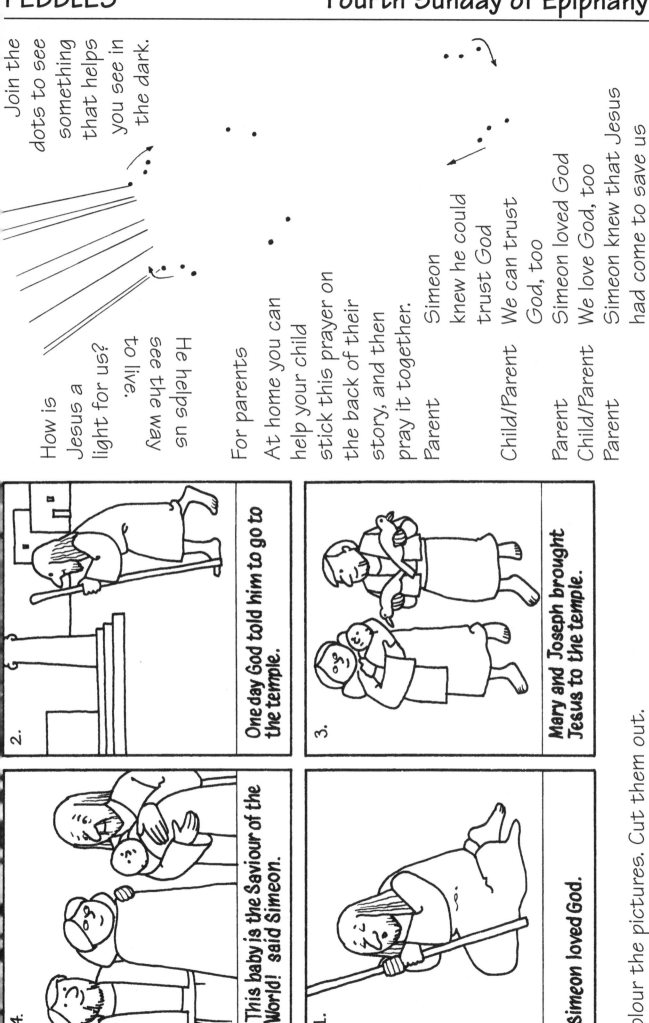

2.

One day God told him to go to the temple.

3.

Mary and Joseph brought Jesus to the temple.

4.

This baby is the Saviour of the World! said Simeon.

1.

Simeon loved God.

Colour the pictures. Cut them out.
Stick them in the right order on a strip of card.
Tell the story.

ORDINARY TIME

PROPER 1

Thought for the day

God calls his people and commissions them.

Readings

Isaiah 6:1-8 (9-13)
Psalm 138
1 Corinthians 15:1-11
Luke 5:1-11

Aim

To introduce them to the story of the catch of fishes.

Starter

Have a fish-catching game, either using magnets on strings and paperclips on the fish, or a bazaar-stall fishing game with floating fish which are caught with hooks. The fish for the magnet game can either be made beforehand or cut out ready and then coloured by the children.

Teaching

Tell the story with the children acting it out as you go along. They can find their way to their boat in the dark, push their boat out, throw out the nets, sit and wait, pull in the nets and shake their heads when they find no fish, throw the nets out again, wait and yawn, pull the nets in, and repeat this until morning comes and they rub their eyes. They can shade their eyes to see all the crowds coming, beckon Jesus and help him into the boat, and sit on the sand to listen. Then they push the boat out again, throw in the nets, wait, and pull them in full of fish! Tell the children how Peter was amazed at what had happened, and a bit frightened by it. Jesus told him he didn't need to be afraid, and invited Peter to follow him. Peter said yes, and spent the rest of his life following Jesus and telling other people about him.

Praying

Sing this prayer to the tune of *One, two, three, four, five, once I caught a fish alive.*

One, two, three, four, five,
Thank you, God, that I'm alive!
Six, seven, eight, nine, ten,
Here I am to help you, then.
What job can I do?

Love God as he wants me to,
showing his love each day
living life the loving way.

Activities

On the sheet the children create a collage picture of the story. You will need some scraps of net curtain or the net bags that oranges come in and some fish cut from shiny paper.

Notes

To make the collage picture

1 Colour the picture
2 Stick on the fishing nets
3 Stick on lots and lots of fish

One, two, three, four, five,
Thank you, God, that I'm alive!
Six, seven, eight, nine, ten,
Here I am to help you, then.
What job can I do?
Love God as he wants me to,
showing his love each day,
living life the loving way.

For parents

Please help your child learn this prayer by singing it together every day.

Cut out and colour this fish and put a paper clip at the mouth. Try catching it at home with a fridge magnet.

What a lot of fish!

PROPER 2

Thought for the day

The challenges and rewards of living by faith.

Readings

Jeremiah 17:5-10
Psalm 1
1 Corinthians 15:12-20
Luke 6:17-26

Aim

To know that we can trust God.

Starter

Chickens. The children run and peck around until the mother hen clucks a danger warning. Whenever that happens, the chickens stop what they are doing and run to the safety of the mother hen (one of the leaders on a rug). When she tells them the danger is over, they can scatter again.

Teaching

Talk about how the chickens know they will be safe with the mother hen. They can trust her to look after them. Talk together about what happens if they fall over and hurt themselves, and draw their attention to the fact that because someone loves them, they look after them. Talk about the way they look after pets and the way they can look after their mums and dads and grandparents with hugs and helping them.

God looks after us all. He has given us a lovely world to live in, with food for us to eat, and all the things we need to make homes and clothes and toys and cars. That's because he loves us.

Praying

When I am afraid
I will trust in you, O God.
I will take shelter under your wings.
(From Psalms 56 and 57)

Activities

On the worksheet there are instructions for making a working model of chickens running to the safety of the mother hen's wings. You will need string and sticky tape, and may prefer to prepare the chicks and hen in card.

1 Colour and cut out
2 Make holes and thread strings.
  Stick strings at back to card
3 When the mother hen clucks,
  make the chicks run to her for safety

We can always trust Jesus

For parents

This prayer can be stuck on
to the mother hen. Pray it
with your child.

When I am afraid
I will trust in you, O God.
I will take shelter
under your wings.
                        Amen.

PROPER 3

Thought for the day

Jesus teaches us to love our enemies and forgive those who sin against us.

Readings

Genesis 45:3-11, 15
Psalm 37:1-11, 39-40
1 Corinthians 15:35-38, 42-50
Luke 6:27-38

Aim

To learn to make up when things go wrong.

Starter

Let the children draw on chalkboards and rub it all out again. Or use the magic writer pads that enable you to erase what you have drawn.

Teaching

Talk about and demonstrate how we can rub out our mistakes on a chalkboard. Draw a nasty splodge as you talk about someone being unkind. But then they say, 'I'm sorry I was unkind.' If someone says that to us we can say, 'That's OK. I forgive you!' As you say it, rub out the splodge.

Jesus says, 'Forgive one another. Pray for those who are unkind to you.' When we do this we are rubbing out the unkindness and clearing the way to start again.

Praying

Thank you, God,
for forgiving me.
Help me to forgive as well. Amen.

Activities

Help the children to make the two finger puppets from the worksheet and fix them on their fingers, so they can practise getting cross and making up again. They can also colour and fold the model on the sheet to see what a difference forgiveness makes.

Colour the pictures. Cut out. Fold along the dotted lines. Now you can swing the middle flap over to make a 'before and after' story.

Colour the finger puppets. Cut out and stick round fingers with rubber bands or sticky tape.

For parents

Ask your child to show you how to put things right when we are unkind and pray this prayer together.

Thank you, God for forgiving me. Help me to forgive as well.   Amen.

SECOND SUNDAY BEFORE LENT

Thought for the day

'He commands even the winds and the water and they obey him.'

Readings

Genesis 2:4b-9, 15-25
Psalm 65
Revelation 4
Luke 8:22-25

Aim

To introduce them to the love of God in his creation.

Starter

Have a hands-on exploration of creation. Provide trays of pebbles, sand, water (protect the surrounding areas or use the washbasins), different textures and different smells. Have books with pictures of animals, birds, fish and insects. The children can wander round touching and enjoying all the different objects.

Teaching

Talk about the different things they have explored and emphasise what a lovely, varied world God has made. Talk about how the world is like a garden God has made, with all these lovely things in it, and all the animals, and people to look after it. Talk over with them how we can look after it well.

Praying

Thank you, God,
for the sun and the rain,
for plants and animals and birds.
And, most of all,
thank you, God,
for making me ME! Amen.

Activities

Give the children paper and paints to celebrate in art our creation and the way God provides for us. Mount the finished pictures and display them with photographs and today's prayer in an area of the church or hall.

Spot the difference

For parents
Pray this with your child and you can both add in the particular things each day for which you are thankful.

Thank you, God, for the sun and the rain, for plants and animals and birds. And most of all, thank you God for making me ME!
Amen.

Sunday before Lent

Thought for the day

God's glory makes Moses' face radiant, and it transfigures Jesus as he prays on the mountain. Our lives, too, can become increasingly radiant as the Spirit transforms us.

Readings

Exodus 34:29-35
Psalm 99
2 Corinthians 3:12-4:2
Luke 9:28-36 (37-43)

Aim

To look at how lives can shine with God's love.

Starter

Patches of sunshine. Have some cut-out circles of yellow paper scattered on the floor and explain that these are patches of sunshine in a dark wood. The children move and dance around to some music, and when the music stops they go and stand on a sunshine patch. Take away a patch each time so that in the end there is only one patch of sunshine left. Children not finding a patch to stand on are out.

Teaching

Talk about how much we need the sunshine. We need God's love to shine in the world too. God can help us to make our lives shine like patches of sunshine in the dark forest. Put out the sunshine patches again, and this time tell the children to stand in the darkness when you say something which is bad or sad, and go to a sunshine patch when you say something good and loving.

Bad and Sad
People hitting and hurting each other
Being grumpy and sulky
Being a pain
People not having anywhere to live
People telling lies
People not having enough to eat

Good and Loving
People saying sorry
Being friendly
Helping someone
People sharing their things with others
People telling the truth
People giving money to buy food for the starving

By physically moving into the sunshine when the 'shining lives' qualities are mentioned, the children will begin to understand the symbolism of radiant light in a spiritual sense. Jesus' life shone because of what he said and what he did. Our lives can shine with his love like patches of sunshine.

Praying

You will need the children to have made their sunshine mats for this. They start by standing on the mat and singing to the tune of *Twinkle, twinkle, little star*. At the darkness section the children move off the mat and walk around it, first one way and then the other, before moving back on to the mat for the last line.

We are sunshine in the darkness,
we are shining with your love.
Help us when we live in darkness,
help us when we live in darkness,
help all those who live in darkness
to shine like sunshine with your love!

Activities

Have some sheets of yellow paper with a wavy outline drawn on. Children old enough to use scissors can cut these out. Others will need help here. Or use white paper and let the children colour them with yellow crayons. The prayer from the sheet can be cut out and stuck on to the mat so that parents can sing the prayer with their children at home. The sheet also includes pictures of Jesus' shining life to colour, and a puzzle to see which behaviours belong to the 'light'.

Notes

Draw in the child Jesus is making better. Then colour the picture.

Draw in Jesus giving the blind man his sight. Then colour the picture.

Cross out the unloving things and colour the sunshine things in bright colours.

Parents: Cut out, stick on the the sunshine mat, and sing the prayer together.

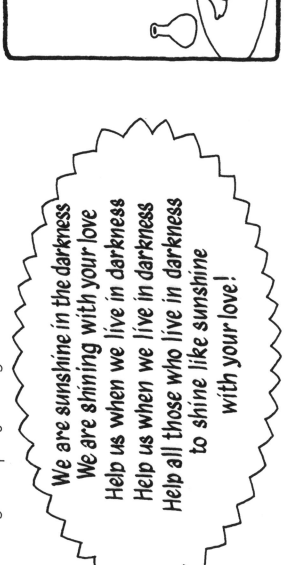

We are sunshine in the darkness
We are shining with your love
Help us when we live in darkness
Help us when we live in darkness
Help all those who live in darkness
to shine like sunshine
with your love!

LENT

FIRST SUNDAY OF LENT

Thought for the day

Following his baptism, Jesus is severely tempted out in the desert, and shows us how to overcome temptation.

Readings

Deuteronomy 26:1-11
Psalm 91:1-2, 9-16
Romans 10:8b-13
Luke 4:1-13

Aim

To look at good ways of living.

Starter

Have a selection of balancing activities for the children to try. These could include walking between two chalk-drawn lines, climbing up to stand on a chair without using your hands, walking along a bench, standing on one leg, and walking along a piece of string laid along the floor.

Teaching

Talk about the balancing acts and how we had to try hard to stop ourselves falling and to keep our balance. In the way we live we have to try hard to do what is kind and loving and good. (Walk along the string line as you say this.) Sometimes we fall down on that (wobble off the string here), and end up being unkind and selfish. When that happens we have to put things right and get back to being kind and loving again. (Go back to walking along the string again.)

Have some pictures of people behaving well and badly. Show the pictures one by one, and decide together whether the people are walking God's way or not. If they are, put the picture on the string; if not, place it away from the string. Copy the pictures below or use your own ideas. They need to be pictures your particular group can relate to.

Praying

To the tune of *Here we go round the mulberry bush*. Act out the verses and add or alter them as appropriate for the group. The children's ideas can be incorporated too.

Help us, God, to share our toys,
share our toys, share our toys,
help us, God, to share our toys,
and live as Jesus told us.

Other verse ideas: to help our mums / help our dads; to look after our pets; to tell the truth

Activities

On the worksheet there is a chart to be filled in through the week to draw attention to their good, brave and honest behaviour, and a 'spot the loving living' activity. They can also be taught Jesus' summary of the law using their fingers. They simply touch each finger of one hand (as if counting) as they say the words 'Love God, love each other'.

Notes

Love God, love each other

To do this week

Monday	Tuesday	Wednesday	Thursday	Friday	Saturday

Colour in a 'thumbs up' when you are

Good   Brave   Honest

For parents

You can sing this prayer to 'Here we go round the mulberry bush'. You can make up other verses too.

Help us God, to share our toys, share our toys, share our toys, help us God, to share our toys, and live as Jesus told us.

Other verse ideas:
to help our mums/help our dads
to look after our pets
to tell the truth.

Talk about the things you spot

Spot the loving living!

SECOND SUNDAY OF LENT

Thought for the day

If only we will agree to put our faith in God, he will fill our lives with meaning and bring us safely to heaven.

Readings

Genesis 15:1-12, 17-18
Psalm 27
Philippians 3:17-4:1
Luke 13:31-35

Aim

To know that God makes promises and keeps them.

Starter

Pass the parcel. In the middle is a key with a promise that says, 'You will be able to give everyone here a sweet.' The key opens a box in which there are sweets for everyone (the right number exactly). The winner of the key gives the sweets out.

Teaching

Talk about how when *(John)* got the key it didn't look much like sweets for us all, but the message turned out to be true. By using the key John did end up with just enough sweets for all of us.

Share some promises the children know about, either ones they have made or those which have been made to them. Talk about what promises are, and how important it is not to break a promise and not to make a promise you can't keep.

God is very good at making promises and he always, always keeps them. The Bible is full of stories about God's promises and how they all came true. So we can trust God, because he means what he says.

And one of his big promises is to you and me. God has promised us that whenever we talk to him he will be listening, and whenever we need him he is there. God doesn't have to go to sleep, so we don't need to worry about waking him up, and he's never too busy to spend time with us.

Praying

Dear God,
I can't see you with my eyes
but I know you are here
because you promised you would be,
and you always keep your promise.
I'm glad you always have time to listen,
and you know what it's like to be me. Amen.

Activities

The worksheet looks at promises and how they sometimes get broken by people. God's promise to Abram is explored, and the children can make a night sky full of stars with dark blue or black paper and stick-on gold and silver stars. The title from the worksheet can be stuck on to the sky picture.

Notes

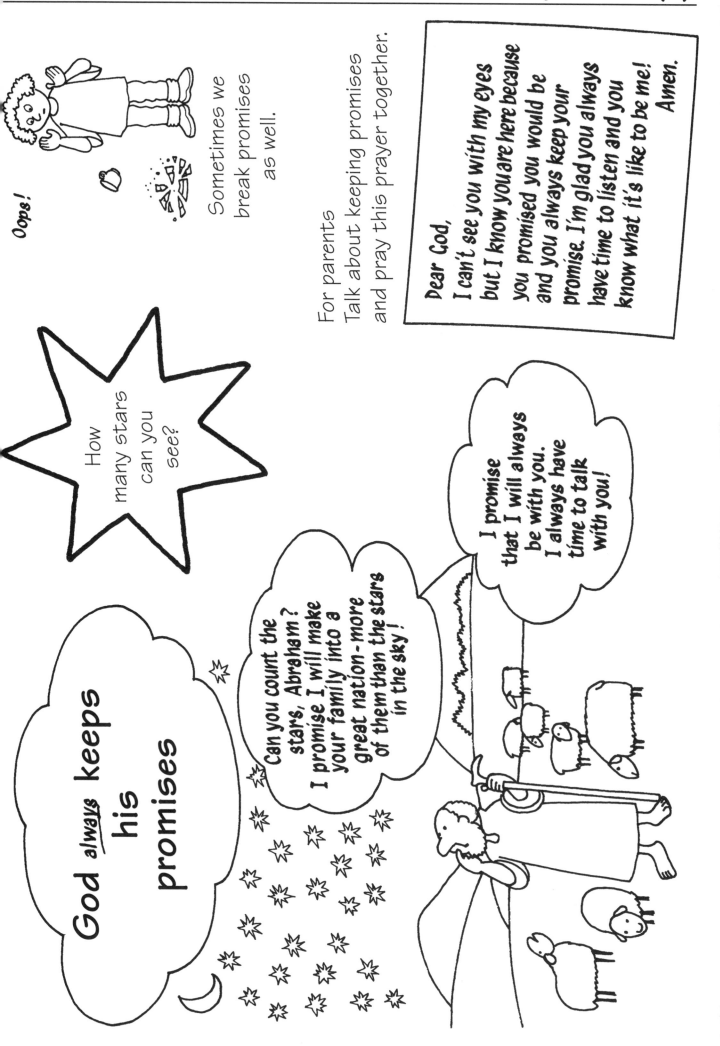

THIRD SUNDAY OF LENT

Thought for the day

We have God's invitation to come and drink freely of his Spirit, but if we keep refusing his offer it will eventually be withdrawn.

Readings

Isaiah 55:1-9
Psalm 63:1-8
1 Corinthians 10:1-13
Luke 13:1-9

Aim

To enjoy the gift of water and thank God for it.

Starter

Water play. Protect the children and the floor and have some bowls of water on low tables, plenty of sieves, and containers, and things that float and sink. Also water some plants and/or give a pet a drink.

Teaching

Talk about being thirsty and needing water. Whether we are plants or animals we all need water to live. Make up a picture of a blue river running through a green field, using coloured paper cut to shape. Put foil fish in the river, plants and trees near the water, foxes and badgers and birds all drinking the water. Stick each item on with a glue stick as you talk about it, and let the children help. You can all admire and talk about the finished picture. Water keeps us all alive. Jesus says, 'You need God like you need water'. This can be written as a title for the water picture, or for very young children the title can be 'Thank you, God, for water'.

Praying

We can drink it, swim in it,
cook and wash up in it,
fish can breathe in it.
What can it be?
It's water! God has given us water!
And we say thanks! *(glug, glug)*
Thanks! *(swish, swish)*
Thanks! *(sizzle, sizzle)*
Thanks! *(splish, splosh)*
Thanks! *(bubble, bubble)*

As the children make the sounds they mime the drinking, swimming, cooking and so on.

Activities

Using the worksheet the children can draw in the different animals, plants and birds on the pictures and discover someone who enjoys water by completing a dot-to-dot puzzle.

Notes

Draw in the trees and flowers that need water to live

Draw in the animals who have come to drink the water

Join the dots to find someone who loves water. Then you can colour him in.

For parents
Pray this together at bathtime.

We can drink it, swim in it,
cook and wash up in it,
fish can breathe in it.
What can it be?
It's WATER! God has given us
WATER!
And we say THANKS! (glug, glug)
THANKS! (swish, swish)
THANKS! (sizzle, sizzle)
THANKS! (splish, splosh)
THANKS! (bubble, bubble).

Thank God for WATER!

FOURTH SUNDAY OF LENT: MOTHERING SUNDAY

Thought for the day

While we are here in this life, given one another to care for, we can learn the lessons of mutual love and support and shared suffering.

Readings

Exodus 2:1-10 or 1 Samuel 1:20-28
Psalm 34:11-20 or Psalm 127:1-4
2 Corinthians 1:3-7 or Colossians 3:12-17
Luke 2:33-35 or John 19:25-27

Activities

Today is not one for learning separately but for celebrating together. Use some of the all-age suggestions from the *Living Stones* Complete Resource Book, and provide shakers and bells for the younger ones to play during one or two hymns, and streamers to wave. Gather the children round the altar for the eucharistic prayer and choose hymns where the language is accessible without an honours degree in English.

Have materials for making cards available for the very young.

Notes

Colour the picture, fold it into a card and have the message written for you inside.
Give it to your mum with a smile and a hug.

Thank you!

Colossians 3:12-17

FIFTH SUNDAY OF LENT

Thought for the day

When we are privileged to share in Christ's suffering, we also share in his new life.

Readings

Isaiah 43:16-21
Psalm 126
Philippians 3:4b-14
John 12:1-8

Aim

To see that God is in the sad and hard times as well as the happy ones.

Starter

Have an assortment of junk, crayons, paint, wool and glue. Tell the children that all this is stuff that no one wants. It's stuff that people have thrown out as rubbish. But we can use it to make things. Set the children free to transform the junk, and then share and admire what we all managed to make.

Teaching

Talk about the fun we've had with some old boxes and thrown-out rubbish. God never thinks of anything or anybody as rubbish. He can make beautiful things out of everything. Show some seed. What does God make out of this dried up, dusty stuff? Flowers! (Show some pictures from a seed catalogue.) Show some vegetable peelings and old tea bags. What can God do with this smelly old stuff? Compost to help the tomatoes grow! (Show some ripe compost.)

It's the same with people. God doesn't think, 'Oh, they're too small for me. I can't work with them.' He thinks, 'Ah, good! Some small people to cheer someone up, or give their mum a hug, or teach the grown-ups. Just what I needed!' And he doesn't think, 'Oh, they're no good to me now they're old and can't get out much.' He thinks, 'Ah, good! Some old people who can't get out much, so they've lots of time to think and pray for the holiday club. Just what I needed!' For God nothing is rubbish and nobody is rubbish.

God can even use the times we are sad. He can even use the bad things like accidents and wars, and make something good come from them. Nothing and nobody is too bad for God to use, because he loves us all.

Praying

Loving God,
I am glad you love us so much.
I am glad I can help you now
as well as when I am grown-up.
You can use my sadness as well as my happy times
whenever you like. Amen.

Activities

If the children need more time to finish their junk models they can do that now. The worksheet helps them think about the good that God can bring out of such things as moving house, a rainy holiday, and a time in hospital. Make sure they understand that God never makes bad things happen to us, but when they do happen he always works to use them for some good.

Notes

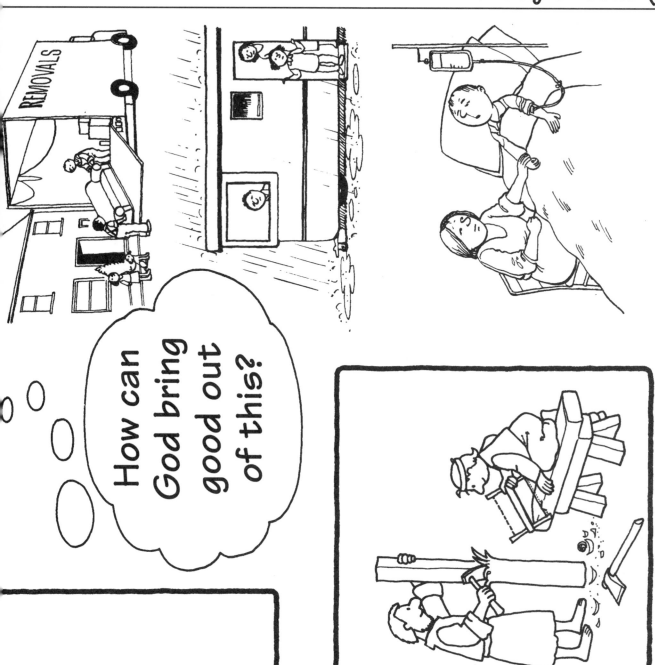

How can God bring good out of this?

Jesus liked making things too

My junk model looks like this

For parents
Pray with your child each night
as you kiss them goodnight.

Loving God,
I am glad you love us
so much.
I am glad I can help you
now as well as when I am
grown up. You can use my
sadness as well as my happy
times whenever you like.
Amen.

PALM SUNDAY

Thought for the day

As Jesus rides into Jerusalem on a donkey, and the crowds welcome him, we sense both the joy at the Messiah being acclaimed, and the heaviness of his suffering which follows. Jesus' mission is drawing to its fulfilment.

Readings

Liturgy of the Palms:
Luke 19:28-40
Psalm 118:1-2, 19-29

Liturgy of the Passion:
Isaiah 50:4-9a
Psalm 31:9-16
Philippians 2:5-11
Luke 22:14-23:56 or Luke 23:1-49

Aim

To introduce them to the story of the entry into Jerusalem.

Starter

Stop, wave, shout hooray! When different signs are displayed the children 'Stop!' (a red circle), 'Wave!' (a cut-out or real palm branch), and 'Shout hooray!' (a crown). You can also sing a praise song, such as *Sing Hosanna*.

Teaching

Using upturned bowls and pots and a green cloth or large towel, let the children help make a model landscape. Boxes covered in white paper make the Jerusalem buildings, and the path down into the Kidron valley is a length of brown crêpe paper or material. Cut out coat shapes of fabric which the children can lay down on the road in front of Jesus, and have a card cut-out of Jesus riding on the donkey which you can move along as you tell the story. Let the children all wave their paper palm branches, standing around the model. They will feel as if they are all part of the story.

Praying

Hooray for Jesus,
riding on a donkey!
Hooray for Jesus,
he is our King!
Hooray for Jesus,
coming to Jerusalem!
Hooray for Jesus,
he is our King!

Activities

Today the children may be joining in the parish procession, with streamer-waving, singing and dancing. They will also be preparing the model. Have large palm leaves drawn on green sugar paper. Older children can cut these out themselves, and those just mastering the scissors technique can make random cuts along the sides of the basic shape. Pictures to help with this and the houses are given on the worksheet. There is also a picture of the event which the children can complete by drawing in the people cheering Jesus on his way.

Notes

Can you help finish the picture?
Draw in the missing bits.
Draw in lots of people, cheering Jesus on.

HOSANNA!

green paper

cut out

Palm branches

boxes

white paper

draw
the
window
and door and stairs

Houses

For parents
Pray this together when you can shake
or jangle keys, or dried peas in a jar.

Hooray for Jesus riding on a donkey!
Hooray for Jesus he is our king!
Hooray for Jesus coming to Jerusalem!
Hooray for Jesus he is our king!

EASTER DAY

If possible, it is recommended that the children and young people are in church with the other age groups today. Use and adapt some of the all-age ideas from the main *Living Stones* book, and involve the children in some of the music and in the decorating of the church.

Thought for the day

It is true. Jesus is alive for all time. The Lord of life cannot be held by death. God's victory over sin and death means that new life for us is a reality.

Readings

Acts 10:34-43 or Isaiah 65:17-25
Psalm 118:1-2, 14-24
1 Corinthians 15:19-26 or Acts 10:34-43
John 20:1-18 or Luke 24:1-12

Aim

To enjoy celebrating that Jesus is alive.

Starter

Have an Easter egg hunt, preferably outside if this is safe and practical.

Teaching

Palm Tree publish a version of the Resurrection story called *Jesus is risen*; or you could tell the story gathered around an Easter garden that the children have helped to make.

Praying

Jesus died for us

arms out, head down

Now he's alive for us

jump up and clap hands over head

Hip, hip, HOORAY!

Jesus is alive today!

raise arms

Activities

Use plasticine or playdough for the children to make their own models of the garden, and the women coming to the empty tomb. On the worksheet there is a picture of the women visiting the tomb early on the first Easter morning.

JESUS IS ALIVE!

Where are the Easter eggs?

Can you find 10 eggs?

For parents
Pray with your child, using the actions.

Jesus died for us (arms out, head down)
Now he's alive for us (jump up and
clap hands over head)
Hip, hip, HOORAY!
Jesus is alive today (raise arms)

SECOND SUNDAY OF EASTER

Thought for the day

Having seen Jesus in person, the disciples are convinced of the Resurrection. We too can meet him personally.

Readings

Acts 5:27-32
Psalm 118:14-29 or Psalm 150
Revelation 1:4-8
John 20:19-31

Aim

To experience that something can still be there even if we can't see it.

Starter

Play a peep-bo game with the younger children and a hunt-the-slipper game with the older ones. Point out that the slipper was there all the time, even before we found it.

Teaching

Spread out a towel, sheet or carpet tiles on the floor and copy the pictures below on to thin card. Gather the children around and tell the story of today's Gospel, using the pictures.

Praying

Dear Jesus,
I can't see you
but I know you are here.
I know you can hear me,
and I know you love me.
Thank you, Jesus! Amen.

Activities

On the worksheet there is a dot-to-dot picture of Jesus to complete, and a picture to colour. Also there is an activity which helps the children appreciate their senses, and realise that sight is not the only way of knowing something is true. Possibilities for the seeing but not touching category would be the sun, moon and stars; hearing but not seeing might be someone's heartbeat, the wind, or thunder; touching but not hearing might be a table or a sandwich; and all three might be a person.

Notes

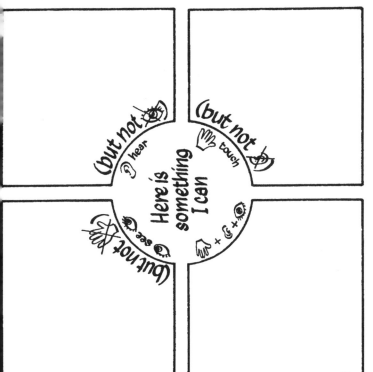

Here is something I can
(but not hear)
(but not touch)
(but not see)

For parents
To pray with your child

Dear Jesus,
I can't see you
but I know you are here.
I know you can hear me,
and I know you love me.
Thank you, Jesus! Amen.

Join the dots to make Jesus appear.

THIRD SUNDAY OF EASTER

Thought for the day

Those who know Jesus and recognise that he is the anointed Saviour are commissioned to go out as his witnesses to proclaim the good news.

Readings

Acts 9:1-6 (7-20)
Psalm 30
Revelation 5:11-14
John 21:1-19

Aim

To get to know the story of today's Gospel.

Starter

Going fishing. Borrow or make the kind of magnet rod and lines which can catch paper fish with paperclips on their mouths. Have the paper fish cut ready so the children can decorate them and add the paperclips. Put the fish in a carton pond, and let fishing commence!

Teaching

Tell the story with the children all acting. They push the boat into the water, throw the net out into the water, wait, inspect the net, wait some more, and get fed up. Then catch sight of a man on the beach, cup your hand to your ear to hear what he says, pull in the net, throw it in the other side and haul in the massive catch. Realise that the man on the beach is Jesus, give a great shout, wade to shore and enjoy breakfast together.

Praying

Dear Jesus,
thank you for coming with us
to the shops/on the bus/to the dentist.
Wherever we go
you are always there for us. Amen.

Activities

If you get enough small cartons, each child can colour one to make a complete fishing set to take home. The worksheet has the outline for a collage picture which can be completed by sticking on cotton wool clouds, shiny paper fish and a red shiny paper fire on the beach. There is also a fish jigsaw with the words 'It's Jesus!' on it.

Colour the fish

It's Jesus!

Cut it out
cut it up.
Do the jigsaw!

For parents
You can adapt this prayer to use wherever you are going, and say it together on the way.

Dear Jesus,
Thank you for coming with us to the shops/on the bus/to the dentist.
Wherever we go you are always there for us.
Amen.

Stick on the fish, clouds sunshine and fire.

cotton wool

yellow shiny paper

fire

Stick on cotton wool

stick on fish

'Come and have breakfast!' shouted Jesus.

FOURTH SUNDAY OF EASTER

Thought for the day

Asked if he really is the Christ, Jesus directs his questioners to look at his life in action and see for themselves that he and the Father are one.

Readings

Acts 9:36-43
Psalm 23
Revelation 7:9-17
John 10:22-30

Aim

To get to know the story of Tabitha being brought to life again.

Starter

Have some simple lace stitching for the children to try. You can make your own sewing cards by punching holes in a greetings card picture, and providing lengths of coloured string with Sellotape wound round the end to make the threading easier.

Teaching

Tell the children that the person in today's story was also very good at sewing. Her name was Tabitha, and she enjoyed getting pieces of material and making them into all sorts of lovely things that people could use and wear. Show them the kind of things Tabitha might have made, such as clothes and sheets. Explain how, when Tabitha got very ill and died, her friends were very sad, and they asked one of Jesus' friends to come to the house. The friend's name was Peter and he came straight away. Tabitha's friends showed Peter the lovely things Tabitha had made, and they told him what a kind person she was, and how sad they were that she had died. Usually people who die go to live with Jesus in heaven, but this time God had another plan for Tabitha.

Now because Peter was such a close friend of Jesus, Jesus could work through him. Peter went upstairs and knelt down beside Tabitha's bed. He prayed and prayed, and then, in Jesus' name, he said to the woman, 'Tabitha, wake up'. And Tabitha opened her eyes and looked at Peter, and smiled! So Peter held out his hand and helped her up. Through Peter, Jesus had brought Tabitha back to life again. It was a sign that Jesus really was alive and working in his friends. And Tabitha's friends were all very happy. They thanked Peter, and I expect Peter said it was God they really needed to thank, so they all hugged Tabitha and thanked God for giving their friend back to them for a while longer. Perhaps Tabitha made Peter something to wear, as a thank-you present. What do you think she might have made for him?

Praying

Dear God,
you are so kind to us,
so good at knowing
what we need.
You are my God and my friend. Amen.

Activities

On the worksheet there is a 'spot the difference' and a 'dot-to-dot' activity to encourage the children to talk about the story. They can also continue or develop the sewing, and have a sewing demonstration by a leader or a visitor from the church. It is important that the children understand that being brought to life is a very unusual event.

Notes

For parents to pray with your child

Dear God,
You are so kind to us, so good at knowing what we need. You are my God and my friend. Amen.

Spot the difference.

What do you think Peter is saying?

Join the dots to see what Tabitha had made.

FIFTH SUNDAY OF EASTER

Thought for the day

Christ, breaking through the barrier of sin and death, allows us to break into an entirely new way of living which continues into eternity.

Readings

Acts 11:1-18
Psalm 148
Revelation 21:1-6
John 13:31-35

Aim

To know that Jesus' friends love one another.

Starter

Sit in a circle and give everyone a chance to talk about their friends – what their names are and what they like playing together. Then play a circle game as friends together, such as 'The princess slept for 100 years', or 'In and out of the dusky bluebells'.

Teaching

Explain that today we are thinking about friends, and we're going to find out about Jesus and some of *his* friends. The children can do all the actions as you talk about the way Jesus and his friends went for walks together, listened to each other (cup hand to ear), talked together (open and close hands to make them 'chat'), laughed together and cried together. They sometimes went to parties and ate nice food together and drank refreshing drinks together. At the end of the day they got tired together (yawn).

Jesus loved his friends and he said to them, 'I want you to love one another like this. Even when you don't feel like it, I want you to be kind to one another and look after one another.' And that's what all Jesus' friends try and do.

Jesus has lots of friends. There are the friends who lived with him in Galilee, and there's all of us who follow Jesus today. We can be his friends as well – when we walk together, listen to each other, talk together, laugh together and cry together. And when we eat and drink, and when we get tired at the end of the day, Jesus is still with us, loving us.

Praying

I have a friend who is deeper than the ocean,
I have a friend who is wider than the sky,
I have a friend who always understands me,
whether I'm happy or ready to cry.

Jesus is my friend who is deeper than the ocean,
Jesus is my friend who is wider than the sky,
Jesus is my friend who always understands me,
whether I'm happy or ready to cry.

Activities

The worksheet has pictures to encourage the children to explore what it means to live in the loving way which marks us out as Jesus' friends, and they can fold, cut out and colour a string of Jesus' friends who are holding hands.

Notes

Pray with your child

I have a friend who is deeper than the ocean,
I have a friend who is wider than the sky,
I have a friend who always understands me,
Whether I'm happy or ready to cry.
Jesus is my friend who is deeper than the ocean,
Jesus is my friend who is wider than the sky,
Jesus is my friend who always understands me,
Whether I'm happy or ready to cry.

Which people are being Jesus' friends

Fold

another

Fold

one

Fold

love

Fold

friends

Fold

My

Sixth Sunday of Easter

Thought for the day

The continuing presence of God, as Holy Spirit, leads us, as Jesus promised, into a personally guided outreach to all nations.

Readings

Acts 16:9-15
Psalm 67
Revelation 21:10, 22-22:5
John 14:23-29 or John 5:1-9

Aim

To introduce them to the idea of going where God the Holy Spirit leads us.

Starter

Follow my leader. Choose several children to take turns at leading everyone around to music, walking, hopping or dancing in the way they choose.

Teaching

Talk together about when we say goodbye, and practise waving to one another and blowing kisses. Talk about feeling sad when the time comes for saying goodbye to friends or grandparents and we don't want them to go.

Explain how Jesus' friends didn't want him to go, and when the time came to say goodbye they were sad. They didn't look forward to being without him. Jesus wanted them to know that he would not be leaving them on their own. The Holy Spirit of God would be coming to be with them and lead them in the right direction.

Praying

As you lead the children through a drawn or marked pathway, lead them also line by line in this prayer:

Spirit of God,
lead me along the paths
of kindness
and love. Amen.

Activities

The idea of leading is continued in the worksheet where they can take their finger for a walk through the country. There is also a matching activity to start you talking about keeping in touch with God so that we know where we are being led. Give the children the opportunity to ask for God's help and guidance in any areas of their life which they are a bit scared about, or which make them sad. Their recording of these places visually will be part of the prayer, and you can talk later about how God answered them. Children need to know right from the start that God can work with them and through them.

Notes

Draw a place where you need God's help to be brave or loving

For parents to pray with your child

Spirit of God, lead me along the paths of kindness and love. Amen.

Match them up!

Some ways we keep in touch

Can you lead your finger all the way round the path?

ASCENSION DAY

Thought for the day

Having bought back our freedom with the giving of his life, Jesus enters into the full glory to which he is entitled.

Readings

Acts 1:1-11 or Daniel 7:9-14
Psalm 47 or Psalm 93
Ephesians 1:15-23 or Acts 1:1-11
Luke 24:44-53

Activities

It is likely that Ascension Day services for schools will not need a separate programme for children. However, I have included a drawing and colouring activity for today so that children in church can work at this during the sermon.

The all-age ideas in the *Living Stones* Complete Resource Book include the following suggestions.

- Any artwork or writing that the children have done on what the Ascension is about can be displayed around the building, and time given in the service to looking at it.

- Have a beautiful helium balloon at the ready. Write on it an Ascension message that the children would like to send. After the service two representative children can let the balloon float away.

- Children can wave white and yellow streamers during some of the hymns.

SEVENTH SUNDAY OF EASTER

Thought for the day

Jesus lives for all time in glory; we can live the fullness of Resurrection life straight away.

Readings

Acts 16:16-34
Psalm 97
Revelation 22:12-14, 16-17, 20-21
John 17:20-26

Aim

For them to know that Jesus is in heaven, and explore what heaven is like.

Starter

Sit in a circle and describe different children and objects by giving clues about them. The children have to guess who or what is being described. (I'm thinking of something that is warm . . . and colourful . . . and has a hole to put your head through. What could it be?)

Teaching

Young children may not have been involved in Ascension Day services so tell them today about the friends of Jesus getting used to seeing him alive after Easter. Now the time has come for Jesus to go into heaven, and his friends won't see him any more. Use pictures cut out of card and move them around on carpet tiles or towels on the floor, with the children gathered round the outside of the landscape. Pictures to copy are given below. Cut out a large cloud to hide Jesus from their sight, and then take the friends back to Jerusalem rejoicing, before you add in the angels welcoming Jesus into heaven.

Praying

The angels said,
'Hallo, Jesus. Well done!'
I want to say it too:
'Hallo, Jesus.
Well done!'
Amen.

Activities

On the worksheet is a pattern for making angels. For the very young these will need to have been already copied and cut out. If you want to have lots of angels for each child use the template and cut the angels from that, perhaps using different colours of paper. Cotton or wool can be attached to the heads either by tying, or with sticky tape. Use shoe boxes for the surroundings of heaven, and white paper with cotton wool on it for the cloud. Use the picture of Jesus from the Ascension Day worksheet.

Notes

Jesus goes up to heaven

You can make lots of angels!

Glue on back b

cut

cut

Welcome, Jesus!

glue

Colour your angel and cut it out. Put wool through the hole. Join (a) to (b)

Draw the person who wears this badge

5 metres swimming

For parents
Pray with your child beside the model.

The angels said,
'Hallo, Jesus, Well done!'
I want to say it too:
'Hallo, Jesus. Well done!'
Amen.

Draw the person who wears the crown

PENTECOST

Thought for the day

As Jesus promised, the Holy Spirit is poured out on the apostles and the Church is born.

Readings

Acts 2:1-21 or Genesis 11:1-9
Psalm 104:24-34, 35b
Romans 8:14-17 or Acts 2:1-21
John 14:8-17 (25-27)

Aim

To celebrate the birthday of the Church.

Starter

Jack in the box. Have everyone crouching down. The leader says, 'Ready, steady, Jack in the box!', and everyone springs up. Vary the length of time between the 'ready' and the 'steady' so the children are hanging on the leader's words, ready to spring into action, but not sure when to.

Teaching

Explain how Jesus' friends had been told to wait for the coming of the Holy Spirit after Jesus had gone into heaven. They were praying and waiting, and waiting and praying for over a week, and then suddenly the Spirit came to them all.

Bring in a birthday cake with two candles on it. If possible, have the cake in the shape of a church, or have a picture or model of a church on it. Explain to the children that today is the birthday of the Church, not just of St Andrew's but all the churches everywhere in the world. Light the candles, each of which stands for about a thousand years. It is now about two thousand years since the Holy Spirit of God was poured out on Jesus' friends and the Christian Church was born.

As you talk about the handing-on of the Gospel, use a set of Russian dolls, and keep taking another one out. Those few people told lots of others about Jesus, and those others told lots more, and their children and their grandchildren, and then the grandchildren grew up and they told their friends and their children and their grandchildren. And soon more and more people all over the world knew about Jesus and the love God has for us. And they went on telling other people until eventually someone told us! So now we know about Jesus and God's love for us, and through our lives we'll tell our friends and our children and our grandchildren so they will know as well.

Sing 'Happy Birthday, dear Church', blow out the candles and share the cake.

Praying

Happy birthday, dear Church,
Happy birthday, dear Church.
Jesus' love is for ever,
Happy birthday, dear Church!

Activities

Have some fairy cakes already iced, and let the children decorate them ready to give out to everyone as birthday cake after the service. The worksheet has a picture to colour of the Church being born at Pentecost.

Notes

ORDINARY TIME

TRINITY SUNDAY

Thought for the day

The unique nature of God is celebrated today, as we reflect on the truth that God is Creator, Redeemer and Life-giver.

Readings

Proverbs 8:1-4, 22-31
Psalm 8
Romans 5:1-5
John 16:12-15

Aim

To help them appreciate the wonder of God.

Starter

Let them make something, such as a picture, from all kinds of bits and pieces, such as wool, bottle tops, toffee wrappers and feathers. Or they can paint or print a picture. This activity needs to be fairly unstructured, so they express themselves in their pictures.

Teaching

Display all the pictures and admire them. Talk about how when we enjoy thinking of things and making them, we are doing what our God loves doing. He loves making things that are beautiful and huge and tiny. He loves making people, and watching over us as we grow and learn to do all sorts of things for ourselves, using the brain he has given us.

Pass round a few things God has made for the children to look at, touch and smell. Talk together about how lovely they are. (You might have a stone, a shell, a feather and a flower.)

Praying

Lord God,
I love the things you have made.
They show me your love. Amen.

Activities

Give the children large letters to colour and stick these with their pictures on to a long roll of wallpaper which can be displayed in church. The finished message reads: 'Our God is wonderful!' The worksheet also has this message, together with a dot-to-dot which again puts them in the role of creator so they can appreciate God as Creator.

Notes

72

Our God is wonderful

God made me, too!

To pray with your child

Lord God,
I love the things
you have made.
They show me
your love.
        Amen.

Thank you God!

Have you ever
seen these?

PROPER 4

Thought for the day

The good news we have been given is not just for us, but to pass on to the rest of the world.

Readings

1 Kings 18:20-21 (22-29), 30-39
or 1 Kings 8:22-23, 41-43
Psalm 96 or Psalm 96:1-9
Galatians 1:1-12
Luke 7:1-10

Aim

To learn how to start spreading the good news.

Starter

Sit in a circle and pass the parcel. Put a Christian sticker in each layer, and a Bible story book in the middle.

Teaching

Talk about the way they have been passing the parcel on, so everyone gets a turn, and how good they were at that. Now we're going to pass our news on to each other, but we don't need to put it in a parcel. We can speak our news and everyone will be able to hear it at once. Have a sharing news session, making sure the children listen to each other by passing a 'talking shell/stone' around. Only the one holding this can speak.

Tell the children that you have a piece of very good news you want to pass on to them. Holding the talking stone/shell tell them that you have found out that God is real and that he loves us all. Following Jesus makes you very happy and helps you live a good life. Ask if any of them know that piece of good news as well.

Tell the children that there are quite a lot of people who don't know this good news yet, and they need people to tell them. What can we do about that?

Write their ideas down. It doesn't matter that they can't read them; they know adults write things down that are important, and will pick up on the truth that their ideas are being taken seriously.

Praying

Lord Jesus,
I am sad that some people
don't know you yet.
Please bless them
and send someone
to tell them about you. Amen.

Activities

This will lead on from the ideas the children have. You may be scribing messages to go with their drawings that can be copied and given to Baptism families, or people being married in your church. You may be making posters to be put up where the slimming and line-dancing classes are held. You may be taping their messages. Have an assortment of materials at the ready.

The worksheet has a 'message delivery' activity, an outline to use for messages, and a 'matching people with message' puzzle.

Notes

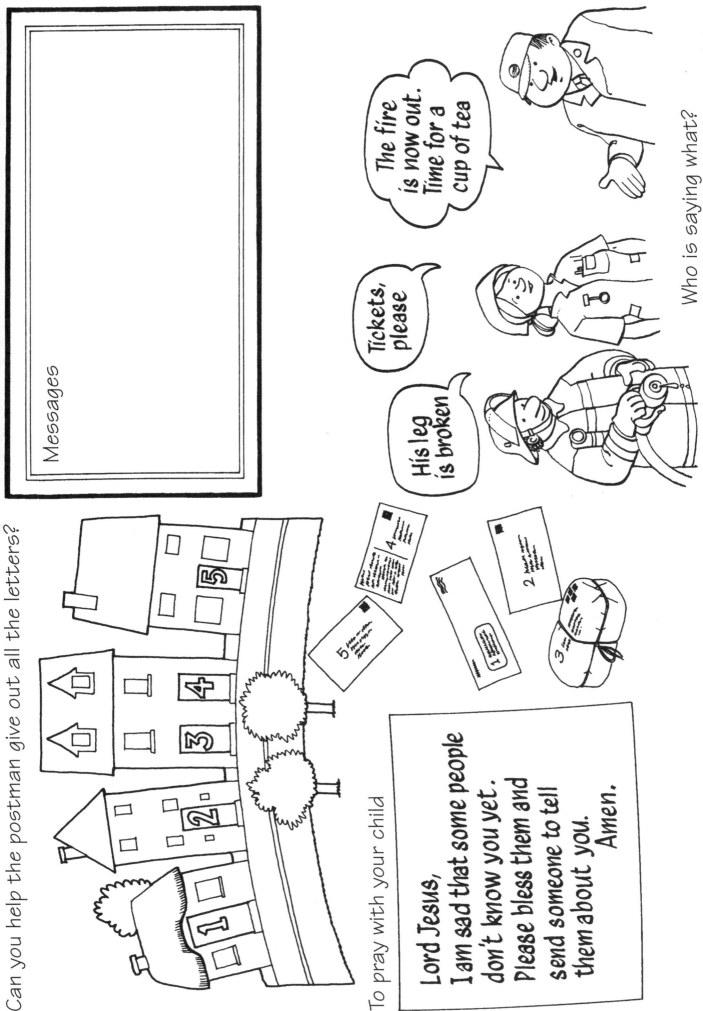

Messages

The fire is now out. Time for a cup of tea

Tickets, please

His leg is broken

Who is saying what?

Can you help the postman give out all the letters?

To pray with your child

Lord Jesus,
I am sad that some people don't know you yet.
Please bless them and send someone to tell them about you.
Amen.

PROPER 5

Thought for the day

Our God is full of compassion; he hears our crying and it is his nature to rescue us.

Readings

1 Kings 17:8-16 (17-24) or 1 Kings 17:17-24
Psalm 146 or Psalm 30
Galatians 1:11-24
Luke 7:11-17

Aim

To get to know the story of the widow at Nain.

Starter

Sad and happy. Make a smiley face for one end of the room and a sad face for the other end. The children find a space in the middle. The leader calls out situations, and if it's something that makes them sad they run to the sad face; if happy, to the happy face. Situations may be eating chocolate, playing with friends, your pet being ill, going on holiday, having a tummy ache, and getting an invitation to a party.

Teaching

Bring the wall labels down and lay them on the floor together, back to back. Today we are going to hear about someone who started off being very sad (show this side) and Jesus helped to make her very happy (show the happy side.)

Tell the story, making sure the children understand what a widow is (otherwise they may assume you are talking about a window). When you tell them about her son dying, ask them how the mother was feeling, and show the sad face. How did Jesus know she was so sad? Let them add these details to the story. Take your time over telling them how Jesus raised the young man to life, pausing for a moment after he has said, 'Young man, get up'. When Jesus gives the young man back to his mother, look at the sad face again. Did the mother feel sad now? Change the face to match her joy.

Praying

Lord Jesus,
we pray for people who are sad.
Please help them to be happy again. Amen.

Activities

Make masks using paper plates with the eyes already cut out. They draw a happy face on one side and a sad one on the other.

Notes

Which is the odd one out?

Draw what the widow cooked for Elijah.

To pray with your child

Lord Jesus,
We pray for people
who are sad.
Please help them to
be happy again.
Amen.

God loves us!

Which things would make Jesus 😊 happy?
Which things would make Jesus 😢 sad?

PROPER 6

Thought for the day

God has the authority and the desire to forgive our sins completely and set us free from guilt.

Readings

1 Kings 21:1-10 (11-14), 15-21a
or 2 Samuel 11:26-12:10, 13-15
Psalm 5:1-8 or Psalm 32
Galatians 2:15-21
Luke 7:36-8:3

Aim

To know that God loves us and forgives us.

Starter

Have a number of sorting-out games, such as getting different shapes into the right holes, sorting out a Happy Families set of cards into families, and tidying a muddle of a cupboard or dressing-up box.

Teaching

Talk about what a good job we did of sorting those things out and putting things right again. Whenever we do that we're being like God, because God loves putting things right and sorting out the messes we make in our lives. Let's look at the sort of things God puts right.

Using toys or puppets, have them acting out various situations where someone is behaving wrongly. For instance, one toy can be greedy and take all the cakes, so there aren't enough for the others; there may be two being nasty to a third, and leaving them out all the time; 'Mum' may leave the children playing, and one keeps kicking or saying nasty things to the other. Vary the situations to suit your group. At the end of each situation let the children say what the wrong behaviour was, and think how they should have behaved. (This may be fun to find out!)

Talk about how we all behave badly sometimes, and the good thing is that, as soon as we realise we have done wrong, we can say 'I'm sorry' to God and 'I'm sorry' to the people we have upset. And then it can be put right straight away so we can get on with enjoying life again.

Praying

Thank you, Jesus,
for showing me
when I was being unkind.
I'm sorry I did it.
Thank you for forgiving me!

Activities

On the worksheet there are examples of unkind and selfish behaviour for the children to talk about, together with an activity to put right what is wrong. Even young children need to be taught about these things. It is important that the teaching is matched with friendly, trustworthy leaders and a secure, loving church environment. The children are invited to think of an area where they know they find it hard to behave well, and draw them doing it God's way. The process of drawing the right behaviour is positive reinforcement and will help develop good self-esteem.

Notes

Me, doing it God's way

To pray with your child.

Thank you, Jesus,
for showing me when
I was being unkind.
I'm sorry I did it.
Thank you for
forgiving me!   Amen.

What's wrong here?

Let's put it right!

Proper 7

Thought for the day

God is close through all our troubles, and can bring us safely through them.

Readings

1 Kings 19:1-4 (5-7), 8-15a or Isaiah 65:1-9
Psalms 42, 43 or Psalm 22:19-28
Galatians 3:23-29
Luke 8:26-39

Aim

To know the story of Jesus healing the man in the desert.

Starter

Make some paper chains, using either the ready-stuck kits or strips of different coloured paper and glue or staples.

Teaching

Wind all the finished paper chains around one of the children, and tell them that today's story is about a grown-up who had to be chained up to keep him from getting into danger.

Tell the story as if you are one (or two) of the villagers. When you mention the way this man had to be chained up, the child can break out of the chains, just as the man did. Get across in the telling that Jesus loved the man and felt sorry for the way he was chained up inside his illness. When the man is healed he can sit still and talk just like we can, and he asks Jesus if he can come with him. But Jesus has a job for him right here in his own town. He can tell everyone what God has done for him. That will make people listen, because they remember what he was like before Jesus healed him.

Praying

Lord Jesus,
thank you for being with us
when we are sad and upset.
Thank you for cheering us up.
Help us to cheer people up
when they are sad. Amen.

Activities

On the worksheet there are bits of a person to be cut out and stuck together on the space provided. Younger children will need these cut out already, and if you prefer you can give the children card 'person chunks' to keep in a clear greetings card wrapper as a jigsaw to make up at any time. There is also an activity to spot the odd ones out, which will draw their attention to the way God asks us to welcome everybody in. With God, no one is left out.

Notes

Make this look like you

Cut it up and put it together like a jigsaw

When we need sorting out, God can do it

To pray with your child

Lord Jesus,
Thank you for being with us when we are sad and upset.
Thank you for cheering us up.
Help us to cheer people up when they are sad.
Amen.

Which is the odd one out?

With God no one is left out

PROPER 8

Thought for the day

When we are called to follow Jesus, that means total commitment, with no half-measures.

Readings

2 Kings 2:1-2, 6-14 or 1 Kings 19:15-16, 19-21
Psalm 77:1-2, 11-20 or Psalm 16
Galatians 5:1, 13-25
Luke 9:51-62

Aim

To understand that we are called to follow Jesus.

Starter

A 'you-do-as-I-do' story. Here is one example. The actions are mostly obvious.
'I'll tell you a story. This story is new,
  so you listen carefully and do as I do.
This is Tom Thumb and this is his house.
These are his windows *(hands make glasses at eyes)*
  and this is Squeaky, his mouse *(your little finger).*
Early one morning the sun began to shine.
Squeaky mouse sat up in bed and counted up to nine.
One, two, three, four, five, six, seven, eight, nine! *(in a squeaky voice)*
Then he took a great big jump and landed on Tom's bed *(your left hand).*
He quickly ran right up Tom's arm and landed on his head.
Squeaky pulled Tom's hair, Squeaky pulled Tom's nose,
till in the end Tom Thumb jumped up and put on all his clothes.
Then they sat down to breakfast and ate some crusty bread.
And when all that was over, Tom Thumb said . . .'
(back to the beginning)

Teaching

Have several chairs in a line, and prepare beforehand card church windows, door and tower clock as shown below.

By name, ask a particular child to sit on one of the chairs and hold a window. Continue to call by name for particular jobs until you have a complete church. Point out that you called them all to do particular jobs, and in doing them the children have become a church.

Jesus calls his followers to jobs that only we can do, and when we agree, and start doing them, we all become the Church of God. This Church isn't really a building, is it – it's a group of people. And that's what the Church is – a group of people called to do God's work in the world.

Praying

Jesus, you have called me
to follow you,
and here I am!
Lead on, Jesus,
I'm right behind you.

Activities

Have a look at the pictures of some jobs people have been called to and talk about them, and people you know who do such jobs. Then they can draw a picture of themselves doing a job that God likes them to do. This may be any kind of caring, thoughtful behaviour.

Notes

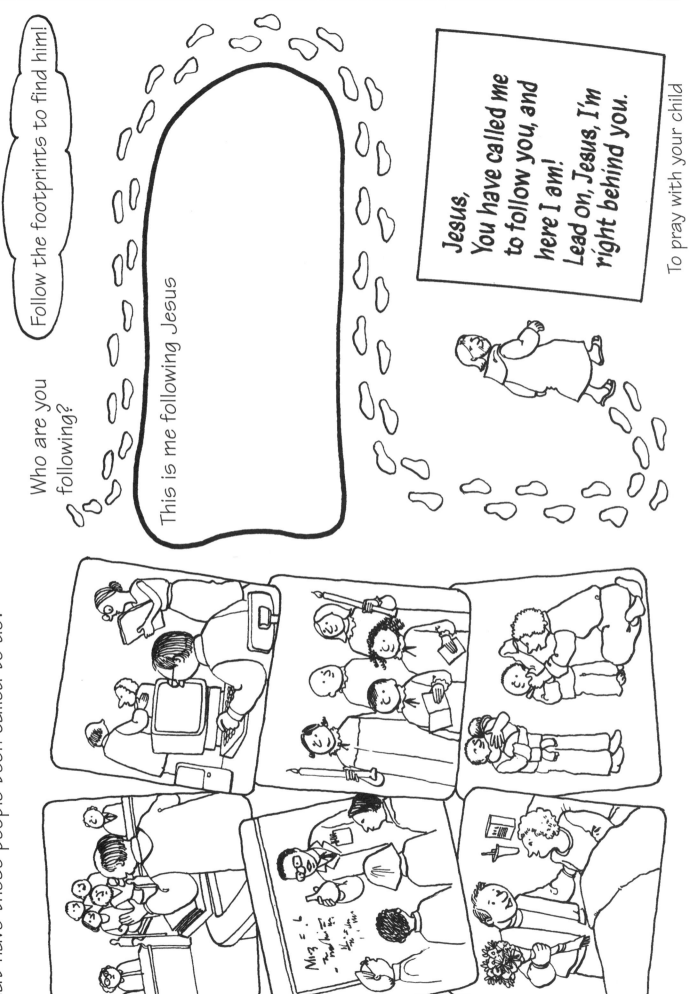

Follow the footprints to find him!

Who are you following?

This is me following Jesus

Jesus,
You have called me to follow you, and here I am!
Lead on, Jesus, I'm right behind you.

To pray with your child

What have these people been called to do?

PROPER 9

Thought for the day

In Christ we become a new creation.

Readings

2 Kings 5:1-14 or Isaiah 66:10-14
Psalm 30 or Psalm 66:1-9
Galatians 6:(1-6) 7-16
Luke 10:1-11, 16-20

Aim

To get to know the story of Naaman.

Starter

Do some magic painting, where the water has the
effect of bringing the invisible colours to life. Split a
book of pictures among the group and provide water
and brushes.

Teaching

The *Palm Tree Bible* series has a version of this story
called *Naaman's Spots*. Either tell the story like this,
sharing the pictures in the book, or enlarge the pictures to show to a larger group. Pictures are available
as line drawings in *Instant Art for Bible People and
Scenes*. Or you could tell the story with a suitably
dressed Action Man as Naaman, washing him seven
times in a bowl of water!

Praying

Lord Jesus,
I pray for all the people
who are sad and lonely.
I know you love them
as much as you love me. Amen.

Activities

The worksheet gives instructions for making a model
of Naaman with and without his spots, so they can
'play the story' at home. Provide a container for the
pieces.

Lord Jesus,
I pray for all the people
who are sad and lonely.
I know you love them as
much as you love me. Amen.

On the 7th dip bring this Naaman
up out of the water!

Can you put in the dots?

Colour this Naaman. Cut him out and stick
him on card. Dip him into the water 7
times. Only bring him out 6 times.

Have this line cut for you

Colour this blue
and stick on to card

PROPER 10

Thought for the day

Straighten your lives out and live by God's standards of love.

Readings

Amos 7:7-17 or Deuteronomy 30:9-14
Psalm 82 or Psalm 25:1-10
Colossians 1:1-14
Luke 10:25-37

Aim

To know the parable of the good neighbour.

Starter

Have a free play session with games such as dressing-up, which encourage the children to play together as well as alongside each other.

Teaching

Tell the story of the good neighbour, involving the children as the characters and helping them act it out. Teach them the summary of the Law to the tune of *London's burning*:

You shall love the Lord your God with
all your heart and all your mind and
all your strength! All your strength!
And love your neighbour,
and love your neighbour.

Praying

Lord Jesus,
with my lips
I can tell you I love you.
With my life
I will show you I love you! Amen.

Activities

The worksheet encourages the children to look at the way people look after others, and there is a picture to finish and colour of the mugged man in the story being looked after by the good Samaritan. Help the children to talk about ways they can be good neighbours.

To pray with your child

> Lord Jesus,
> Help me to be kind
> and helpful, and use my
> strength to make a
> better world.   Amen.

Colour this picture of the man being looked after by a kind person.

Add a

a

and a

Draw the child being looked after

What has happened here?

What goes in here?

MILK

PLASTERS

Proper 11

are objects drawn for which they can make the sounds, and the picture of a park encourages them to imagine what sounds they would hear if they were in that place.

Thought for the day

Against impossible odds God has reconciled us to himself, in Christ.

Readings

Amos 8:1-12 or Genesis 18:1-10a
Psalm 52 or Psalm 15
Colossians 1:15-28
Luke 10:38-42

Aim

To look at the value of listening.

Starter

Play this game in which they have to listen carefully to the instructions. You give them an instruction of where to move to, followed by the way to do it, such as: 'Go to the front wall as aeroplanes; go to the back wall as window cleaners.'

Teaching

Get everyone to find their ears, and talk about what they are for. Try covering and uncovering ears to hear the effect, notice how loud it sounds if you rub your own ear, but if someone else does it to theirs you can hardly hear it at all. Enjoy the gift of hearing and listening that God has given us, and share your favourite sounds. Think about what sounds you hear when you first wake up.

Then do some exercises to train your listening. Sit very still and listen to all the sounds around for a minute, then share what you heard. Whisper something very quietly and see if you can hear it (it might be something funny, or an instruction to touch their toes with their hair). Have a 'news time', with everyone listening carefully to whoever is speaking.

Tell the children about the way all the grown-ups and children used to come out and listen to Jesus, because they found what he said so helpful.

Praying

Thank you, God,
for my ears to listen with.
Help me to get really good at listening
to you and to other people. Amen.

Activities

Have a tape of different sounds and see if the children can guess what they are. On the worksheet there

Notes

Can you make these sounds?

This is my favourite sound

For parents to pray with your child

Thank you God for my ears to listen with. Help me to get really good at listening to you, and to other people.

Amen.

If you were here, what would you hear?

PROPER 12

Thought for the day

Keep asking for God's Spirit and he will keep pouring out his blessing on you.

Readings

Hosea 1:2-10 or Genesis 18:20-32
Psalm 85 or Psalm 138
Colossians 2:6-15 (16-19)
Luke 11:1-13

Aim

To know that we can ask God for things, and seek him.

Starter

Play hide and seek, either with people, or hunting for a shoe.

Teaching

Talk about asking for things from our parents. If you asked for some bread, would they give you a stone? If you asked for fish and chips, would they give you snake and chips? If you asked for an egg, would they give you a scorpion? You can laugh together over these, and they will see that although they might look a bit alike, their parents would give them what was good for them, not something that was bad for them. Why? Because their parents love them.

Explain that one day Jesus was teaching the people to pray, and he looked at how good parents are at giving good gifts to the children they love. Well, he said, it's just the same only more so with God. He is a very loving parent to all his children, and we can trust him never to give us anything that would be bad for us.

Jesus wants us to ask him about things, and to ask for his help, and to ask for the things we need. If we ask for something that might not be best for us at the moment, he will probably say, 'No' or 'Not yet'. As we learn to ask for things that he wants for us as well, we shall find that he often says, 'Yes, I'd like that too.' He might even ask our help in getting things done.

Praying

Our Father in heaven,
please give us
all we need today. Amen.

Activities

On the worksheet there are activities to reinforce the asking, seeking and knocking. They can also make a model of an opening and closing door.

SEEK   ASK   KNOCK

KNOCK

Cut along the dotted line. Then you can knock and open the door

Can you find 6 ⬭ hidden in this picture?

For parents to pray with your child

Our Father in heaven, please give us all we need today.   Amen.

Proper 13

Thought for the day

True richness is not material wealth; true security is not a financial matter.

Readings

Hosea 11:1-11 or Ecclesiastes 1:2, 12-14; 2:18-23
Psalm 107:1-9, 43 or Psalm 49:1-12
Colossians 3:1-11
Luke 12:13-21

Aim

To know that God looks after us like a loving parent looks after a young child.

Starter

If you have a parent who would be willing to bath a baby with the children there, that would be lovely. Or play a matching parents and babies game. Give each child the picture of an animal, and they have to go round the room looking for the baby picture that matches their adult animal.

Teaching

Talk about the different ways in which the people who love us look after us. On the worksheet there are some pictures to start you off. Tell them how God said to his people, 'I love you like that!' Teach them this song, sung to the tune of 'Three blind mice' and putting in all the children's names.

God loves Oliver.
God loves Louise.
God loves Jordan.
God loves Daisy.
He knows when they're friendly
   and when they get mad,
he knows when they're happy
   and when they are sad,
if they help each other it makes him feel glad,
'cos God loves us!

Praying

Dear Jesus,
your love makes me rich.
Thank you for giving me
so much love to love with!

Activities

The worksheet gets the children thinking of three people they love, and drawing what they would like to give them if they could give them anything at all. This will help them to pray for their three people, and help develop their ability to think in out-giving mode. If you have a garden or outside area they can gather some small flowers (daisies, buttercups, dandelions and bindweed are fine) and make a posy of them in wet cotton wool and foil to take into church and lay as thank-offerings in front of the altar. They can take their flowers home with them afterwards.

Notes

For _____

with love

For parents to pray with your child

Dear Jesus,
Your love makes me rich.
You are my shepherd, and
so I have all I need.   Amen.

When we like giving
we are behaving like God.
He likes giving us
good gifts.

God looks
after us like a
loving parent

Draw what you
would like to
give three people
you love

For _____

with love

For _____

with love

How babies and toddlers are looked after by those who love them

Talk about

You can
colour the
pictures

PROPER 14

Thought for the day

Have faith in God, and get yourself ready to meet him.

Readings

Isaiah 1:1, 10-20
Psalm 50:1-8, 22-23
Hebrews 11:1-3, 8-16
Luke 12:32-40

Aim

To know that God can be trusted.

Starter

Play 'Simon says'. Point out that we had to make sure we only listened to Simon's instructions. We knew if we did that we wouldn't get it wrong.

Teaching

Bring a clock along, with the time an hour fast. Bring one of those pop-up toys which you press down and they suddenly surprise you by popping up before you expected.

As you start, pretend to have just noticed the time on the clock and the time gives you a shock – it's already time we were in church! Then you check with your watch and are very relieved that the clock must be wrong. You know you can trust your watch because you checked that against the television just before you came out.

Talk about there being some things you get to know you can trust, and other things let you down. Share stories about car breakdowns, toys that break, and so on.

We can trust God because he doesn't have 'off' days or go into a sulk. He doesn't move away just when you're getting to know him, and he doesn't go away on holiday. He doesn't have times when you can't get in touch with him. He's always there for us and always fair and loving. So we can trust God with all our fears and our hopes and dreams, all the things that upset us and all the things we're looking forward to. We can trust him with our secrets. He will stay our friend right through to when we're grown up, right to when we get old and even when we've died – he'll still be our friend. By the time we die we will have got to know and love him very well, and he will welcome us into heaven to enjoy being with him for ever.

Praying

Dear Jesus,
it's good to know
I can trust you.
You are always there for me.
Thank you!

Activities

If you can borrow a parachute, you can play some games which build trust and co-operation – working together to make a ball bounce high, and creating a 'mushroom' shape and running underneath it one by one. Or help one another to complete a floor jigsaw. The worksheet gives them space to create a composite picture of themselves and their life, putting in such things as their favourite colours and animals, pastimes and people.

Notes

Dear God, this is me

Draw or stick on things you like – colours, food, and things you like doing

Which could you sit on?

Dear Jesus,
it's good to know
I can trust you.
You are always
there for me.
                    Thank you!

For parents to pray with your child

PROPER 15

Thought for the day

When we fix our eyes on Jesus our lives will reflect his nature.

Readings

Isaiah 5:1-7 or Jeremiah 23:23-29
Psalm 80:1-2, 8-19 or Psalm 82
Hebrews 11:29-12:2
Luke 12:49-56

Aim

To learn that God likes us and wants the best for us.

Starter

Pass the parcel. Make sure everyone has a turn (if necessary, have several parcels with several small groups). Each layer contains a freezer label with 'I'm special' written on it. Eventually every child is wearing one.

Teaching

Pass round a flower each for the children to hold, and talk together about what it is like – what its petals and leaves look like, what it smells and feels like, and so on. Marvel over all the care that God has taken in bringing a flower like this into being.

Now pass round something else to enjoy and notice, such as feathers, stones or vegetables. Again draw their attention to all the care God has taken over these things.

Collect everything in and say we've got another collection of beautiful, amazing things God has made. Get everyone to stand up in the circle and hold hands. At the moment they are making a sort of chain, but they aren't daisies. At the moment they are quiet, but they can speak. What – or who – can they be? It's us!

Sit everyone down and go round the group picking out one nice thing about everyone, and then enthuse together over the loving care God has taken over each one of us. No wonder God likes us and thinks us all very special.

Praying

Thank you, God,
for making me
and knowing me
and liking me.
It's special being special!

Activities

Make finger-print pictures, using shallow trays of paint and hand-washing bowls between colours. Some suggestions for making their prints into people and objects are given on the worksheet.

Notes

My finger-print picture

This is me on my special day

Some ideas

Why is this day special for Oliver?

Why is this day special For Anne and Mike?

Thank you God for making me and knowing me and liking me. It's special - being special !

For parents to pray with your child

PROPER 16

Thought for the day

God sets his leaders apart to challenge prejudices and assumptions, and alert people to the truth.

Readings

Jeremiah 1:4-10 or Isaiah 58:9b-14
Psalm 71:1-6 or Psalm 103:1-8
Hebrews 12:18-29
Luke 13:10-17

Aim

To know that God loves us right from before we were born and all through our lives, and he has a plan for us.

Starter

Moving in style. The children move around the room in the ways that the leader calls out. They can roll like little babies, crawl like older babies, be learning to walk like toddlers, jump and skip like children, ride bikes like older children, ride skateboards like teenagers, drive cars and lorries like grown-ups, and walk with a stick like elderly people.

Teaching

Talk about the way we went right through a person's life in the game. Go over the stages with them, getting the children to remember what they were and helping them get the order right. Out of all those ages in our life, when is it that God loves us? Is it when we're babies? Or when we've grown up? Or when we're old?

God loves us in *all* the ages, because he loves us *all* the time! Right from before we've even been born, God knows us and loves us. Tell the children that God loves them now, and he'll still be friends with them and loving them when they get old and perhaps have grandchildren of their own. Ask them to think of the oldest person they know. God loved all these people right back when they were tiny babies, and even before that!

Praying

You can sing and dance this prayer

Oh, oh, oh how good is the Lord, (3)
I never will forget what he has done for me.

He loves all the babies, how good is the Lord (3) . . .

He loves all the toddlers, how good is the Lord (3) . . .

He loves all the children, how good is the Lord (3) . . .

He loves all the teenagers, how good is the Lord (3) . . .

He loves all the grown-ups, how good is the Lord (3) . . .

He loves the old people, how good is the Lord (3) . . .

Activities

Draw round the children on sheets of lining paper or wallpaper. The children can then colour themselves in. Write across the paper person, 'God has got a plan for me!'

Notes

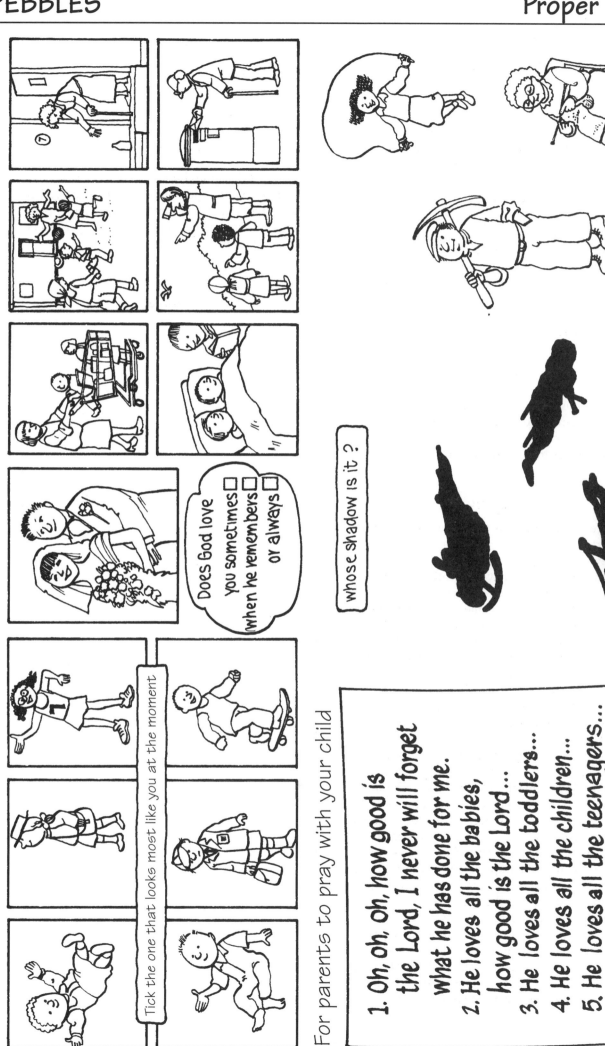

Tick the one that looks most like you at the moment

Does God love you sometimes ☐ when he remembers ☐ or always ☐

whose shadow is it ?

For parents to pray with your child

1. Oh, oh, oh, how good is the Lord, I never will forget what he has done for me.
2. He loves all the babies, how good is the Lord...
3. He loves all the toddlers...
4. He loves all the children...
5. He loves all the teenagers....
6. He loves all the grown-ups...
7. He loves the old people...

PROPER 17

Thought for the day

When we live God's way, both individually and as a community, we will be greatly blessed.

Readings

Jeremiah 2:4-13 or Ecclesiasticus 10:12-18
Psalm 81:1, 10-16 or Psalm 112
Hebrews 13:1-8, 15-16
Luke 14:1, 7-14

Aim

To know the story of the guests choosing the most important seats.

Starter

While the music plays, pass round a grand hat or a crown. Whenever the music stops, whoever is wearing the hat or crown stands up, and all the others bow and curtsey to them, saying, 'Yes, your majesty; no, your majesty!'

Teaching

You can either use puppets to tell the story today, or an assortment of character toys, some of which are very new and posh, while others are well loved, old and tatty. Lay a low table with a cloth and plates of drawn food, and arrange all the chairs around it. One by one the characters come in, talking to themselves about the party, and admiring the food.

One of the new, posh ones looks to see which the most important seat is, and decides to sit there because they are *so important*.

One of the old and tatty well-loved ones comes and looks for the lowest, least important seat, because they are conscious of being old and worn, and not very grand.

When the host comes in they go to the old, worn one and give him a big hug, really pleased that he has been able to come to the party. They ask him to come up and sit with them at the top of the table, as he's so important, having been such a good friend for years. When they get to the top of the table the hosts find the posh guest sitting there and ask them to move down so their special guest can sit there instead. The posh guest voices her embarrassment as she moves down and the old worn one takes his place at the top of the table.

This story teaches us not to think we're far more important than anyone else and deserve better than anyone else. Instead of rushing for the best place, or the biggest cake, or the first go, sometimes we need to enjoy giving the best to other people.

Praying

Big and small,
short and tall,
you made us all,
you love us all! Amen.

Activities

On the worksheet the children are putting the guests in the right places, and the food on the plates. Also, they can paint or model some food on a paper plate to remind them of the story. Today's prayer can be written out on the back of the plate.

Notes

Colour the guests, cut them out and stick them at the right place for the party. Draw in their food.

Jesus invites us to be his friends

For parents to pray with your child

Big and small
short and tall
you made us all,
you love us all!
        Amen.

Proper 18

Thought for the day

Following Jesus is expensive – it costs everything, but it's worth it.

Readings

Jeremiah 18:1-11 or Deuteronomy 30:15-20
Psalm 139:1-6,13-18 or Psalm 1
Philemon 1-21
Luke 14:25-33

Aim

To know that it is worth the cost to follow Jesus.

Starter

Play shops, with play money, boxes and cartons, cut-out fruit and some paper bags.

Teaching

Talk about going shopping, and what they like buying and what they don't like buying. Talk about how we sometimes see things we would like, but we can't have them because they cost too much.

Tell the story, with the aid of a few appropriate props, of a child who sees a toy she really loves and would like for her birthday. Her mum tells her that she won't be able to have it as it costs too much money. The child keeps thinking about the toy, and decides she wants it so much that she doesn't mind not having any other presents, and no birthday treat, if that means she can have it. Her mum and dad talk it over with her. They don't want her to choose to do without those things and then be upset when she has only got one toy. The child is certain that this toy is worth it, so her mum and dad arrange for her to have the toy she wants so much. And the child is so happy with this one thing that she doesn't mind having no other presents and no birthday treat.

Following Jesus is really wonderful. It's wonderful having Jesus as our friend and knowing he loves us all the way through our life and wherever we travel to. But when we follow Jesus, we choose to do without some things.

We choose to do without being selfish, even when we want to be. We choose to do without being unkind, even when we feel grumpy. We choose to do without wanting things all the time, even if we like them.

But it's worth doing without these nasty things, because being with Jesus makes us so happy.

Praying

Jesus, I love you
and I will live like you,
even when it is easier not to. Amen.

Activities

On the worksheet there is a picture to colour of Jesus with the children, and the children can draw themselves in the picture.

Notes

Match real money
with these coins, and
make rubbings of some
real coins, too.

For parents to pray with your child

Jesus, I love you
and I will live like you
even when it's easier
not to.   Amen.

PROPER 19

Thought for the day

Jesus does not avoid the company of sinners but befriends them.

Readings

Jeremiah 4:11-12, 22-28 or Exodus 32:7-14
Psalm 14 or Psalm 51:1-10
1 Timothy 1:12-17
Luke 15:1-10

Aim

To know the story of the good shepherd and the lost sheep.

Starter

Hide and seek, using a model sheep.

Teaching

Let the children help make a landscape from upturned bowls draped with a green sheet or towel. Use model sheep, either plastic ones or home-made from thin card and cotton wool. Bushes and shrubs can be small house plants in pots, such as spider plants and money trees.

When the landscape is set up, tell the story, moving the sheep around as you talk about the normal daily routine for the shepherd caring for his flock, and the lost sheep being found and brought safely home.

Praying

Good shepherd,
thank you for looking after us.
Help us to look after each other. Amen.

Activities

The children can make sheep masks using the instructions on the worksheet, and search for lost sheep in a picture which can then be coloured in.

Can you find the lost sheep? How will the shepherd get to it? Colour the picture

How to make a sheep mask

cotton wool

cut out

punch hole

cut

paper plate

cut along here

Cut shape from a paper plate; draw on the face, cut eye holes and stick on cotton wool. Secure round the head with wool.

To pray with your child

Good shepherd, thank you for looking after us. Help us to look after each other.   Amen.

Proper 20

Thought for the day

If you cannot be trusted with worldly riches, or even small amounts of money, then you will not be trusted with spiritual riches either.

Readings

Jeremiah 8:18-9:1 or Amos 8:4-7
Psalm 79:1-9 or Psalm 113
1 Timothy 2:1-7
Luke 16:1-13

Aim

To learn that we are to be good 'caretakers' and look after things as well as people.

Starter

A potato and spoon game. For each small group of children (2-4 in a group), place a bowl at each end of the room. In one of the bowls there is a potato and a spoon. The first person carries the potato in the spoon from one bowl to the other. The next carries it back to the first bowl, and so on. They can all have two turns. This can either be competitive or simply an activity which several groups happen to be playing at the same time, depending on the age of the children.

Teaching

Talk about how careful they all had to be to walk along holding the potato in the spoon without it falling off. Think how careful we have to be carrying a bowl of cereal, or a drink of juice. We have to really think about what we are doing. If we start thinking about something else, we can end up spilling it all over the floor!

Jesus told his friends that God takes great care making us and looking after us, and he wants us to take great care of things as well. Show a picture of different age groups working or playing together. He wants us to look after one another. (How?) Show a globe. He wants us to look after our world. (How?) Show a toy and a jacket. And he wants us to look after any things we are given to use or play with. (How?)

Praying

Dear God,
thank you for all the things I have been given
to use and to play with.
Help me to look after them well
and be ready to share them with others. Amen.

Activities

There is space on the sheet for the children to draw the things to use and to play with that they like most, and some pictures of things being looked after well and badly, so they can develop their understanding of what good stewardship means.

Notes

Here are some children playing. Colour the ones who are looking after their toys and cross out the ones who are not

These are the things I like to use and play with most

Dear God,
thank you for all the things I have been given to use and to play with.
Help me to look after them well and be ready to share them with others.   Amen.

To pray with your child

PROPER 21

Thought for the day

Wealth can make us complacent so that we fail to notice the needs of those around us.

Readings

Jeremiah 32:1-3a, 6-15 or Amos 6:1a, 4-7
Psalm 91:1-6, 14-16 or Psalm 146
1 Timothy 6:6-19
Luke 16:19-31

Aim

To know that we are to notice one another's needs.

Starter

Spot the difference. The children hide their eyes while you change something (you might take a shoe off, or swap your watch to the other wrist) and then they have to guess what is different.

Teaching

Tell a story about a child noticing someone's need. Here is one possibility:

Emily and her dad were doing the shopping. It was the big weekly shop in the supermarket to get things like toothpaste, cocoa-pops, toilet paper and bread. Emily had got the list, and Dad was pushing the trolley.

The shop was full of people, some of them filling plastic bags with apples and potatoes, and others trying to work out the cheapest way to buy cheese. They were so busy with what they were choosing to buy that no one noticed a sticky white line on the floor by the cat food.

At least, nearly no one noticed. Emily saw it and wondered what it was. As she went to find the rabbit and chicken flavour (her cat's favourite) she followed the sticky white trail, and smelt the smell of concentrated washing liquid. So that's what it was! Emily could see the trail disappearing round the corner into the lemonade and coke part of the shop.

'Dad!' said Emily. 'Look!'

Dad looked.

'Mmm, well spotted, Emily,' he said. 'We had better follow that trail and find out why it's there.'

'It's concentrated washing liquid I think,' said Emily.

'I think you could well be right,' said Dad.

They pushed their trolley round the corner. There, just between the large bottles of lime and lemon and the small bottles of blackcurrant and apple was a woman pushing a trolley. And on the front of the trolley was a refill of concentrated washing liquid, leaking white sticky stuff along the floor as the trolley went along. Anyone could slip over on it and hurt themselves.

Emily and her dad showed the woman the white sticky trail.

'Oh good heavens, fancy that!' said the woman. 'Fancy me not noticing! What a good thing you noticed it before anyone hurt themselves.'

Dad and Emily smiled at each other.

The woman and Emily and her dad told the shop assistants and helped them mop up the mess with paper towels. The manager put down some orange cones saying 'Wet floor' on them, so people would know it wasn't safe to walk there yet.

Talk about how good it was that Emily noticed, and share any stories the children want to tell about times they have noticed when people need help.

God wants us to notice things and be ready to come to the rescue.

Praying

Dear God,
use our eyes
to see the needs around us
and use our hands to help. Amen.

Activities

On the sheet there is a picture on which to spot various needs, and a pair of glasses to make.

Notes

Can you make some pipe-cleaner glasses?

To pray with your child

Dear God,
use our eyes 👁 👁 to
see the needs around us 🖐
and use our hands 🖐
to help.

Amen.

These are the hands I mean!

What do they need?

How could
we help?

PROPER 22

Thought for the day

God hears our distress and our crying, and feels it with us.

Readings

Lamentations 1:1-6 or Habakkuk 1:1-4; 2:1-4
Lamentations 3:19-26 or Psalm 137, or Psalm 37:1-9
2 Timothy 1:1-14
Luke 17:5-10

Aim

To learn about perseverance.

Starter

Have some buckets and beanbags, so the children can try throwing the beanbags into the buckets.

Teaching

Make up an obstacle course which a soft toy, such as a bear, could negotiate with a bit of help from his friends. This might include something high to balance along, a dark tunnel he must hurry through on his own, and something to climb up.

Make a bear walk the obstacle course, talking to himself in a growly voice as he goes along. He is sometimes scared and anxious by the height, sometimes frightened and sad about being alone in the dark, and sometimes finding it all an uphill struggle. There are also parts of his journey with fun and excitement and good views. Through all the difficult parts the bear bravely perseveres. The children can applaud him when he eventually reaches the end of the course.

Talk about how the bear kept on going, even when he was scared or tired. That's what God wants us to do in life.

Praying

Make a ring of string which everyone holds and passes through their hands as they pray:
Lord, help me to keep trying
again and again and again!
Lord, help me to keep loving
on and on and on. Amen.

Activities

On the worksheet there is an obstacle course for the children to make their fingers walk along, and a 'keeping on and on' game to make, for which they will need string.

To pray with your child

Lord, help me to keep trying,
again and again and again!
Lord, help me to keep loving,
on and on and on!

Amen.

Get some

Cut it

Tie it

Fix on
a flag

Make
your flag
go up
and down

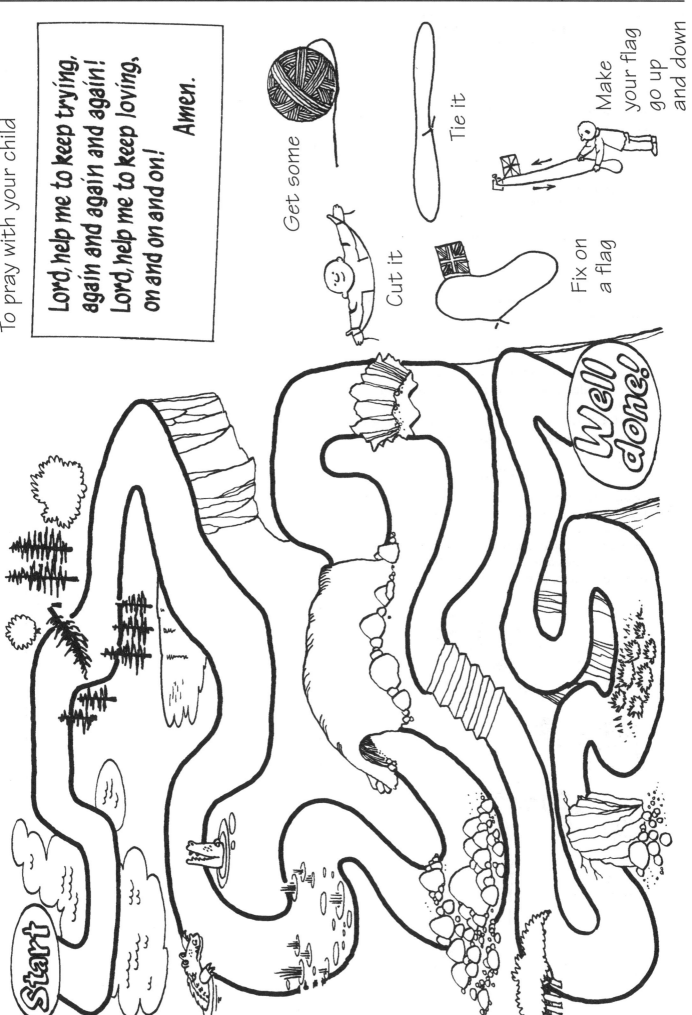

Start

Well done!

Proper 23

Thought for the day

God can always use even seemingly hopeless situations for good.

Readings

Jeremiah 29:1, 4-7 or 2 Kings 5:1-3, 7-15
Psalm 66:1-12 or Psalm 111
2 Timothy 2:8-15
Luke 17:11-19

Aim

To know that Jesus healed the ten lepers and one said 'thank you'.

Starter

Provide a selection of sorting-out games and toys, such as building something from a jumble of bricks or boxes, putting shapes in the right holes, and jigsaw puzzles. Today we are going to look at the way Jesus sorted out ten problems all at once!

Teaching

Using the carpet tiles surface, tell the story of today's Gospel. You will need cut-outs of the lepers, a distant village, some trees, Jesus, the priest, and the leper who said 'thank you'. You can base them on the pictures below. The road to the village can either be a cloth, or strip of paper.

Praying

When we are sad *(chin in hands)*:
you cheer us up *(trace big smile with finger)*.
When we cry *(fists in eyes)*:
you brush our tears away *(brush face with hands)*.
When we feel weak *(go droopy)*:
you make us strong *(show muscles)*
and we say THANK YOU! *(shout)*

Activities

There is a picture of the lepers throwing off their bandages happily when they are healed which the children can colour, after they have counted the lepers and various other things.

Notes

To play with your child

When we are sad (chin in hands)
you cheer us up (trace big smile with finger)
When we cry (fists in eyes)
you brush our tears away (brush face with hands)
When we feel weak (go droopy)
you make us strong (show muscles)
and we say:
                    THANK YOU!

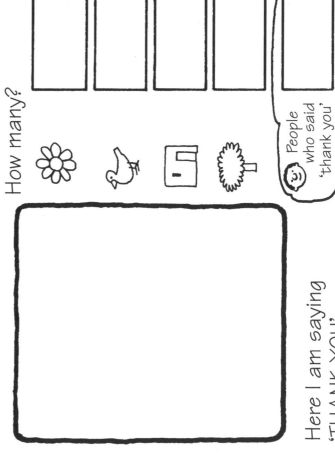

How many?

People who said 'thank you'

Here I am saying 'THANK YOU'

PROPER 24

Thought for the day

Don't get side-tracked; always pray and don't give up.

Readings

Jeremiah 31:27-34 or Genesis 32:22-31
Psalm 119:97-104 or Psalm 121
2 Timothy 3:14-4:5
Luke 18:1-8

Aim

To look at the value of regular prayer.

Starter

Here we go round the mulberry bush. With one of the regular morning jobs being: 'This is the way we pray to God on a cold and frosty morning'.

Teaching

Bring a large circle of card split into the four seasons, and a circular band of paper showing the regular events of a day, based on the pictures below.

Turn the chart round like a wheel, and talk about the seasons and the way the same thing happens every year. Then point out that the days all have a pattern as well. Move the band round so that they can see the same pictures coming up day after day. There are some things we do every day.

Jesus tells us that we should make praying part of our daily pattern too. Have the praying picture, and stick it on the band in the morning, before eating, and before sleeping. Then turn the whole thing round a few times so they get the idea of the ongoing pattern.

Praying

When I wake up I say:
Good morning, Jesus!
Help me live your way today.
When I sit down to eat I say:
Thank you for this food.
Before I go to sleep I say:
Goodnight, Jesus.
Thank you for looking after me.

Activities

The worksheet helps them make their own day's band to use, and there is some pictorial teaching on how to pray.

Notes

Cut along here

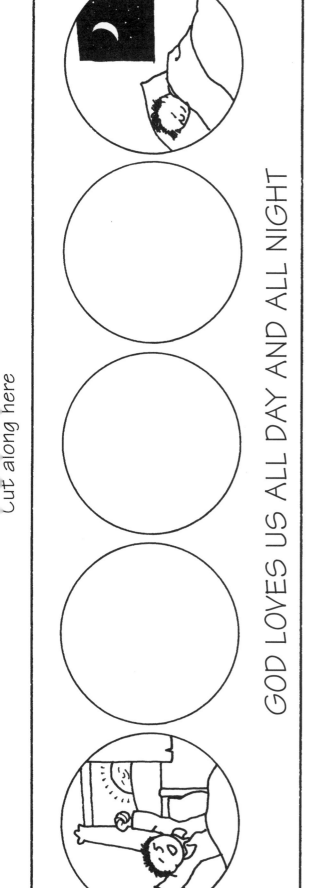

GOD LOVES US ALL DAY AND ALL NIGHT

Cut along here

Draw in what you do each day. Colour all the pictures. Cut the strip out and stick the ends together

You can thank God for your life

You can praise God, who made us all

You can enjoy being with him

What can I say when I pray?

To pray with your child

When I wake up I say:

Good morning, Jesus! Help me live your way today.

When I sit down to eat I say:

Thank you for this food.

Before I go to sleep I say:

Goodnight, Jesus. Thank you for looking after me.

PROPER 25

Thought for the day

When we recognise our dependence on God we will approach him with true humility and accept his gifts with joy.

Readings

Joel 2:23-32 or Ecclesiasticus 35:12-17 or
Jeremiah 14:7-10, 19-22
Psalm 65 or Psalm 84:1-7
2 Timothy 4:6-8, 16-18
Luke 18:9-14

Aim

To know that we are to let God into our life as the earth lets in water.

Starter

Play with water and have lots of sponges, so they can try transferring water from one container to another using the sponges' soaking and water-holding quality.

Teaching

Have a tray of dry earth, and point out how nothing will grow in it if it stays as dry as this all the time, because things need water to grow. We can't grow any goodness in our lives if we don't get showered with God's love.

But that's all right, because God is always there showering us with his love. As you talk, shower the earth with a watering can. He gives us a beautiful world to live in, fruits and vegetables and animals and families to enjoy and look after. He gives us life, and minds to think with, and bodies to move around with.

All the time we keep ourselves open to God like this earth is open to the water, he can fill our lives with his love and we will grow more and more loving and truthful and good.

Praying

Thank you, God,
for the rain that falls.

make fingers into falling rain

Thank you for trees
that grow so tall.

stretch up

Thank you for this life
you have given us all!

move and dance about

Activities

Use the wet earth to plant some bulbs to be ready in the spring. The worksheet has a picture to colour and add the raindrops. Provide raindrops cut from shiny blue and silver wrapping paper for this.

Notes

Stick on the raindrops

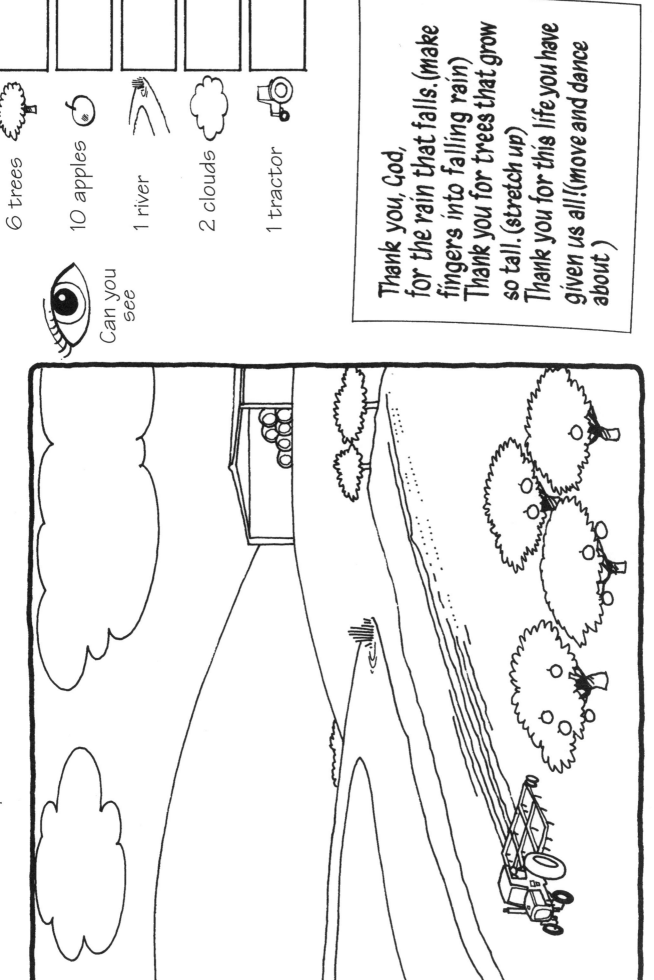

Can you see

6 trees

10 apples

1 river

2 clouds

1 tractor

Thank you, God,
for the rain that falls. (make
fingers into falling rain)
Thank you for trees that grow
so tall. (stretch up)
Thank you for this life you have
given us all! (move and dance
about)

To pray with your child

ALL SAINTS' DAY

Thought for the day

In Christ we are chosen to be God's holy people.

Readings

Daniel 7:1-3, 15-18
Psalm 149
Ephesians 1:11-23
Luke 6:20-31

Aim

To find out what saints are and why we are celebrating today.

Starter

Give out balloons to throw and catch.

Teaching

Talk about the balloons and how much better they are with air inside them. Although we can't see the air we know it is there because the balloons get bigger when you blow air into them. We can't see God's love, either, but when it fills us we grow into loving people. We need God's love in us.

There is a name for people who have spent their lives being filled with God's love. We call them Saints. Saints are close friends of God who want to live God's way so much that they don't mind what happens to them so long as they can carry on being friends with him. Some saints have bravely stood up for what is right. Some have spent their lives looking after the very poor, or those with dangerous illnesses. Some saints have helped lots of people to know and love God better.

Today is like a party to celebrate all the saints, and thank God for what he can do in our lives.

Praying

Sing *Oh, oh, oh, how good is the Lord,* dancing to it in a circle.

Thank you, God,
for your friends, the saints.
Help us to get to know you more
and enjoy being your friends.

Activities

They can make the worksheet into a pop-up picture of the saints cheering us on our way to heaven.

* Hymns Old & New, No. 397; Children's Hymn Book, No. 164.
Both published by Kevin Mayhew Ltd.

TO HEAVEN

cut

fold

fold

cut

To pray with your child

Thank you, God, for your friends, the saints. Help us to get to know you more and enjoy being your friends.

Draw yourself here. Cut it out and stick it on the road. See all the saints cheering you on

Fourth Sunday before Advent

Thought for the day

Jesus came to search out the lost and save them. Through him we come to our senses and make our lives clean.

Readings

Isaiah 1:10-18
Psalm 32:1-7
2 Thessalonians 1:1-12
Luke 19:1-10

Aim

To be introduced to the story of Zacchaeus.

Starter

Spot the birds. Fix a number of bird pictures high up around the room. Show the children an example of what they are looking for, and set them off hunting for the pictures, but don't tell them they will have to look up to see them. Let them discover that for themselves.

Teaching

Prepare the tree by fixing a card or thick paper tree outline to a chair, so that when Zacchaeus stands on the chair you can just see his face over the top of the tree. Give Jesus and Zacchaeus head-dresses to wear, and have all the other children standing at the side of the road as Jesus comes walking through their village. Let Zacchaeus lead Jesus and his friends across the room to his house (some chairs can make the walls) where they sit down to eat. Then they can come outside for Zacchaeus to announce to all the people waiting outside that he is changing his life. He's going to stop cheating people out of their money, and pay back all his debts four times over. All the people can give him three cheers and a round of applause.

Point out that although Zacchaeus was short, he wasn't too short to work with God. They may be short, but they are not too short or too young to work with God either.

Praying

Look, Lord,
I may be short
but I am not too short
to be your friend.
I want to be in your team
and work with you today.

Activities

They can all make a tall tree with Zacchaeus in it to remind them of the story. You will need a length of wallpaper for each child, cut into a trunk, and the tree's crown.

Notes

Stick this to the back of the tree

Stick the tree on and paint it

Glue

Sponge

Paint

Look, Lord, I may be short but I am not too short to be your friend. I want to be in your team and work with you today.

To pray with your child

THIRD SUNDAY BEFORE ADVENT

Thought for the day

Life after death is not wishful thinking but a definite reality.

Readings

Job 19:23-27a
Psalm 17:1-9
2 Thessalonians 2:1-5, 13-17
Luke 20:27-38

Aim

To know that Jesus told us life goes on after death.

Starter

Place some tiny cakes decorated with chocolate drops in a box or tin, and have an extra packet of chocolate drops with you. Tell the children that there is something nice in the tin. Can they see it, without taking off the lid? No. Do they trust you to tell them the truth? (I wonder!) Do they believe that there really is something nice in the tin?

Assure them that there really is something nice in it, and you are going to give them a little idea of what it is like. Now give each child a chocolate drop to enjoy. What do they think is in the tin? Well, it's certainly something to do with chocolate drops. Open the tin so they can all see. It's like chocolate drops but even better, because there's a whole cake, decorated with a chocolate drop for everyone. Now you can give them out one by one, so that everyone has one.

Teaching

When Jesus was walking about on our earth he told his friends that life goes on after our bodies wear out and die. He told them heaven was a nice place to be, and they would be very happy there. (As you say this, hold the closed tin.)

Can we trust Jesus to tell us the truth? Yes, we can.

So if Jesus said there is life after we die, and people are happy there, can we believe him? Yes, we can.

What will it be like? (Pick up the empty packet of chocolate drops.) Jesus gives his friends some clues, and he lets us feel the joy and happiness and peace and love of heaven sometimes. Heaven will be like that only much, much better!

Praying

Be near me, Lord Jesus, I ask thee to stay close by me for ever and love me I pray. Bless all the dear children in thy tender care and fit us for heaven to live with thee there.

Activities

There is a dot-to-dot angel to complete, and then they can draw and paint heaven in their favourite colours. If you want to make this a collage picture, bring along an assortment of different colours and textures for them to use.

Notes

Heaven goes

...n and ...n

...n and ...n

To pray with your child

Be near me, Lord Jesus, I ask thee to stay close by me for ever and love me I pray. Bless all the dear children in thy tender care and fit us for heaven to live with thee there.

I think heaven might look like this

SECOND SUNDAY BEFORE ADVENT

Thought for the day

There will be dark and dangerous times as the end approaches, but by standing firm through it all we will gain life.

Readings

Malachi 4:1-2a
Psalm 98
2 Thessalonians 3:6-13
Luke 21:5-19

Aim

To know that God is a fair judge.

Starter

Weighing and sorting games, using lots of different items, such as stones, vegetables, pasta, bricks, saucepans and feathers. Sort according to shape, use or colour. Use balance scales, or hang two baskets at either end of a broom handle and hold it in the middle. The children can try to balance the baskets.

Teaching

Using toys or puppets, act out several situations which are not fair. Tell the children to shout out 'That's not fair!' as soon as they spot something which isn't. Then talk about why it isn't fair, and act out the same situation, this time making it fair. Here are some ideas for situations:

- Three sweets are shared out between three toys with one toy having two sweets and one having none.

- It's clearing-up time and one toy is allowed to carry on reading while the others have to do all the tidying up on their own.

- The toys are playing 'catch' and one says he hasn't been caught when really he has.

Our God always judges justly, or fairly. He always knows both sides of the story, and he is always fair. So we can trust him.

God has made us able to tell what is fair, so that we can play fairly and grow wise, choosing to do what is right and just. God wants us to stand up for what is fair. He doesn't want people to treat each other badly and unfairly.

Praying

Dear God,
you are a good judge.
You are always fair.
Help me to be fair as well.

Activities

They can make their own set of balances to use at home. They will each need two yoghurt pots, wool, and half a pea stick. The worksheet gives instructions.

Notes

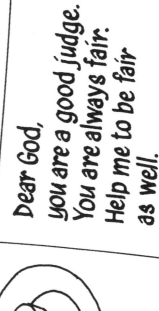

Dear God,
you are a good judge.
You are always fair.
Help me to be fair
as well.

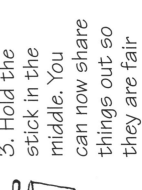

Share the
cakes out
so it is fair

To pray with your child

How to make a pair of SCALES

You will need:
2 yoghurt pots
2 lengths of wool
a pea stick

1. Tie the ends of the
wool to the pots to
make a handle

2. Loop the handles over
the ends of the peastick
and tape them down

3. Hold the
stick in the
middle. You
can now share
things out so
they are fair

CHRIST THE KING

Thought for the day

This Jesus, dying by crucifixion between criminals, is the anointed King of all creation in whom all things are reconciled.

Readings

Jeremiah 23:1-6
Psalm 46
Colossians 1:11-20
Luke 23:33-43

Aim

To know and celebrate that Jesus is our King.

Starter

Scatter different coloured and named circles all over the floor, one for each person. Everyone starts by standing on their own circle. When the music starts, everyone moves and dances around. When the music stops, they go and stand on their spot. A matching set of named circles (small ones) are in a basket, and one is drawn and that person is given a crown to wear. When the music starts this time, everyone follows what the King or Queen does. The crown is changed each time the music stops, and you can easily give everyone a go by removing their name from the basket once it has been chosen.

Teaching

Hold the crown and talk about what kings are often like in fairy stories, establishing that they are usually the most important person in the kingdom, with lots of power and lots of money.

As Christians, we belong to a kingdom. It's a kingdom of love and joy and peace and goodness and forgiveness. Anyone in any country can be part of this kingdom, if they ask to be. It's a kingdom which grows bigger and bigger as more people get to meet with God. And our King is someone who was born in a stable, and died on a cross, and came back to life again. Do you know his name? Yes, it's Jesus. And if we are part of the family of God, which we are, that means we are princes and princesses in the kingdom of God!

Praying

Dear Jesus,
you are my friend
and yet you are a King!
I am glad I live
in your kingdom.

Activities

The worksheet can be decorated and turned into a crown, which the children can wear as they sing some songs to celebrate, such as:

- *Who's the king of the jungle?*

- *I rejoice in making Jesus happy*

- *I'm H - A - P - P - Y*

- *If you're happy and you know it*

Notes

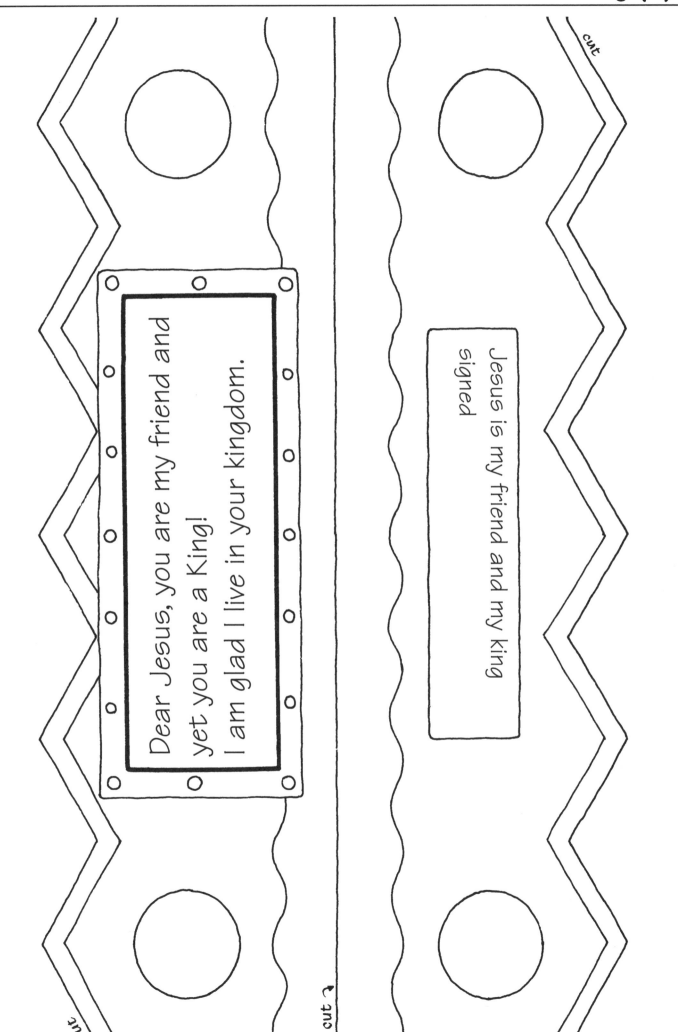

Dear Jesus, you are my friend and
yet you are a King!
I am glad I live in your kingdom.

Jesus is my friend and my king

signed

cut

cut

cut

cut